AF885219

How to Drive Fusebox 5.5

Jeff Peters

Proton Arts – Manassas VA USA

How to Drive Fusebox 5.5

Copyright © 2008 by Proton Arts

FIRST EDITION: September 2008

All rights reserved. No part of this book may be reproduced or transmitted in any form or by any means, electronic or mechanical, including photocopying, recording, or by any information storage and retrieval system, without written permission from the publisher, except for the inclusion of brief quotations in a review.

02 01 00 09 08 9 8 7 6 5 4 3

ISBN 0-9752647-6-1

Interpretation of the printing code: The rightmost double-digit number is the year of the book's publication; the rightmost single-digit number is the number of the book's publication. For example, the printing code 04-1 shows that the first publication of the book occurred in 2004.
Published in the United States of America

Trademarks

All terms mentioned in this book that known to be trademarks or service marks have been appropriately capitalized. Proton Arts cannot attest to the accuracy of this information. Use of a term in this book should not be regarded as affecting the validity of any trademark or service mark. ColdFusion is a registered trademark of Adobe, Inc. Fusebox is a registered trademark of Fusebox, Inc.

Warning and Disclaimer

This book is designed to provide information about CFML programming. Every effort has been made to make this book as complete with respect to its topic and as accurate as possible, but no warranty of fitness is implied.
The information is provided on an as-is basis. The author and Proton Arts shall have neither liability nor responsibility to any person or entity with respect to any loss or damages arising from the information contained in this book or from the use of the programs that may accompany it.

This book was written and set with OpenOffice.org 2.4.1

Dedication

For Elizabeth

As you embark on your own explorations in IT and the world of bits and pixels, I wish for you the joy I've had in traveling that world since before you were born, and the hope that it will take you places I can't even imagine. You are amazing, Monkey.

– Daddy

About the Author

Jeff Peters is a project manager and application architect for NCI Information Systems, Inc. Jeff has been involved in information systems in one way or another since 1973, when he first crash-landed a lunar module on a teletype terminal to the Dartmouth University mainframe. That same machine predicted that he would one day be either a shepherd or President of the United States. Neither of these seems to have been fulfilled.

Involved in the Internet since the late '80s, Jeff was unfortunately working on mainframe projects (taking a hiatus from networked systems) when the 'Net went public and changed the face of application delivery forever. Some days he thinks he still hasn't caught up, but he's found that writing books is a good way to keep in practice. Jeff has written or co-authored eleven books on web development and writing for techies, and has contributed to publications such as ColdFusion Developer's Journal and PocketPC Magazine. His web-development-oriented web site, GrokFusebox.com, provides a gateway to a wide variety of resources. Jeff can be reached at jeff@grokfusebox.com.

Acknowledgments

As always, a number of people have gone into the production of this book. It never happens overnight, and it's never as easy as it seems it should be—even after 11 books. I'd like to thank Sean Corfield for his tireless efforts on Fusebox 5 and 5.5. He's not only been a great asset to the community, but an intellectual inspiration as well. I can remember when he was dead-set against Fusebox, but he had the integrity to give it a fair hearing. Would that we all were so inclined. As this goes to press, Sean has handed the Fusebox coordinating developer reins to Adam Haskell, who also deserves recognition for his contributions.

I'd also like to thank the Fusebox community at large, for their patience in waiting for this book. I had intended its release about a year before it actually came out, but in a way I'm glad it took this long. Fusebox 5.5.1 is significant, and the intervening time has allowed a lot of exploration by the community, and myself as a member of it.

Of course, there's the usual gang of suspects when it comes to the editing, reviewing, and production process—you know who you are.

As always, best and most thanks are to God, by whose hand all good things are done. I can only hope this is one of them.

Jeff Peters
September 2008

Table of Contents

Chapter 1 - Introduction

As this book is going to press, Fusebox is approaching its 10th anniversary. First unleased upon the world in 1998, it has grown to become the most widely used framework in the ColdFusion development community.

While the basic tenets of Fusebox, such as centralized request management and separation of code according to purpose, have remained throughout its history, the nature of Fusebox's implementation has changed quite a bit over the years. Starting out as a collection of best practices and a few custom tags, Fusebox has grown through several iterations of core files, arriving finally at this current version, Fusebox 5.5.

Fusebox 5.5 is quite different from any Fusebox before it, and yet it will make Fusebox developers of practically every stripe feel right at home. More advanced by far than Fusebox 4, more flexible by far than even Fusebox 5, Fusebox 5.5 provides a variety of ways to approach the structure of a Fusebox application, each of them familiar to some segment of the Fusebox community. We hope this book will go a long way toward opening the power of Fusebox 5.5 to you.

About This Book

Many developers struggle to launch projects on time and under budget without staying up all night to do it. Those of us who are successful often wonder how we can improve our success rates. We need advice about communicating with our clients. We need a standard process to make the project manageable. We need a framework to serve as a base for our applications so we stop reinventing the wheel every time. We need a system that simplifies maintenance and requests for change during development.

We need Fusebox.

This book is about making ColdFusion applications reliably successful by following a standardized system. Fusebox is not a new creation. In answer to the problems plaguing software development over the last few decades, the framework described here has been used by thousands of developers to build tens of thousands of applications.

Unlike previous Proton Arts books about Fusebox, though, this one does not cover the Fusebox Lifecycle Process (FLiP), the methodology that is typically used to develop Fusebox-based projects. Instead, this book concentrates on the particular characteristics of the Fusebox 5.5 framework core files and how they can be used in various ways, depending on the skill sets and preferences of the developer. Readers who are interested in FLiP are encouraged to read *Fusebox 5 & FLiP: Master-Class ColdFusion Applications*, by Jeff Peters.

The Fusebox framework also includes guidelines to follow regarding file naming, directory use and file content. While these techniques will be seen in the examples in this book, they will not be discussed in detail, since Fuseboxers are already familiar with them. This book will focus specifically on the features that Fusebox 5.5 brings to the table.

What Is This Book About?

This book provides information on the mechanics of implementing applications with the Fusebox 5.5 framework. It is not an introduction to Fusebox.. As such, this book will cover the following topics:

- A quick overview of Fusebox principles

- Demonstration of a modern Fusebox application

- New features in Fusebox 5.5
- Examples of various ways to approach the organization of a Fusebox 5.5 application.

These topics are intended to stimulate exploration of the variety of ways Fusebox 5.5 can be used to help solve application development problems. Fuseboxers who have typically produced procedurally-oriented applications will have an opportunity to explore object-orientation in part or in full, and all Fuseboxers will have an opportunity to see an application implemented in ways they probably haven't considered before.

What Is This Book Not About?

As noted previously, this book is specifically about how Fusebox applications can be implemented using the Fusebox 5.5 framework. Consequently, it does not address wider issues in Fusebox and/or general web development. This book is not about:

- How to program in ColdFusion. This book assumes you understand basic ColdFusion constructs and principles. If you are not familiar with such tags as `<cfinclude>`, `<cfoutput>` and `<cfswitch>`, check out one of the excellent books available specifically devoted to ColdFusion programming.
- The details of Fusebox best practices. There are already great references available for Fusebox in general.
- The FLiP methodology.
- Interface design, Ajax, Flash, Flex, or the soup du jour. These decisions are left to the individual developer. Again, there are many great references available for these topics.

So who should be reading this book?

Who Should Read This Book?

This book is designed to teach you Fusebox 5.5, so it's a good idea to have some Fusebox experience before jumping in with this book.

If you are an HTML developer and want to create your first dynamic application using ColdFusion, then this book is probably not where you want to start.

If you are an intermediate-level ColdFusion developer who has created a few applications but are planning ahead for the next big, scary project, then this book may or may not be for you. If you learn well from examples and like to explore on your own, you'll probably get a lot out of it. On the other hand, if you prefer to know the "why" of things you're learning, you'd probably be better served by starting with a reference on general Fusebox and FLiP.

If you are an experienced Fusebox developer, then this book is definitely for you. You will have a chance to explore all the variations that can be used with Fusebox 5.5, by far the most flexible and adaptive version of Fusebox so far. If you want to see how other Fuseboxers might approach the same problem set, you will find it here.

Chapters and Flow

This book is arranged so as to guide you through an exploration of what we term "modern Fusebox" (that is, Fusebox 4 and later). We'll start out with a chapter on how a modern Fusebox application is configured. Then we'll look at how Fusebox 5.5 allows us to operate under a wider set of boundaries than we previously had, engaging in such heretical behavior as deleting the fusebox.xml file, for example. After some this sort of wild-eyed roaming, we'll spend several chapters exploring how we might implement the same application using different architectural assumptions. These chapters include things like CFCs for object orientations, CFCs are circuits, and hybrid applications.

The last part of the book some of the added features in Fusebox 5.5, including dynamic <do> verbs, the event object, and using the debug trace.

We'll wrap up with a summary and a few appendices that provide information on the Fusebox XML files and where to find more Fusebox resources, among other topics. The chapters run like this:

Chapter 1: Introduction – you're reading it now!

Chapter 2. Fusebox Basics – A quick overview of the "what and why" of Fusebox.

Chapter 3. "Traditional" modern Fusebox – Reviews the Fusebox 4 approach to Fusebox, using XML to configure the application and circuits.

Chapter 4. Going XML-Less – Issues related to using Fusebox without the XML files, and how Fusebox 5.5 goes about it.

Chapter 5. Other New Topics – Additional features added in Fusebox 5.5.

Chapter 6. Directories as Circuits: Circuit.xml – The Wegot Widgets reference application using directories for implicit circuits and circuit.xml.

Chapter 7. Directories as Circuits: CFML Templates as Fuseactions – The Wegot Widgets reference application using directories for implicit circuits and CFML templates for fuseactions.

Chapter 8. Directories as Circuits: CFCs as Fuseactions – The Wegot Widgets reference application using directories for implicit circuits and CFCs for fuseactions.

Chapter 9. CFCs as Circuits – The Wegot Widgets reference application using CFCs for implicit circuits and CFC methods for fuseactions.

Chapter 10. Summary – The last roundup.

Appendix A: Fusebox Glossary – Useful terms for Fuseboxers.

Appendix B: Fusebox XML Syntax Guide – If you're going to use it, here's a guide.

Appendix C: Fusebox Resources – Websites, blogs, and even other books.

Summary

So that's the basic plan of the book. Rather than providing a complete overview of the Fusebox and the Fusebox Lifecycle Process, this book is designed to provide some insight into the new approaches to Fusebox that are available with Fusebox 5.5. If you're interested in an in-depth treatment of Fusebox, you should have a look at the other titles in the Proton Arts Fusebox collection. Now on with the good stuff...

Chapter 2 – Fusebox Basics

To explain what Fusebox is, let's look first at what it is not. Fusebox is not a commercial software package; there is nothing to buy. Fusebox is also not a development environment or a compiler.

However, Fusebox *is* a web development specification combined with an application framework. People who use Fusebox (*Fuseboxers*) use a standardized development framework to help their projects succeed. Fusebox has the strongest and most dynamic community of ColdFusion developers on the Net today.

Where Fusebox is a framework, the Fusebox Lifecycle Process (FLiP) is a methodology—a set of steps that can be followed to successfully build an application. Fusebox does not require the use of FLiP, nor vice versa.

What is Fusebox all about in practice? There are two major aspects of Fusebox:

1. Basic concepts of the purpose of Fusebox

2. Fundamental Fusebox principles in practice

Each of these aspects is made up of other pieces, so let's take them one at a time.

Basic Fusebox Concepts

Fusebox borrows many of its essential concepts from other systems. First, Fusebox is a way to organize program code. Second, Fusebox is a way to manage growing applications by organizing the application directories in a hierarchy. Third and perhaps most fundamentally, Fusebox is a way to think about applications and the art of building them. Comparisons have been drawn between the Fusebox core files and computer networks. Now let's discuss each of these essential concepts in more detail.

A Way to Arrange Code

A great deal of thought has gone into the idea of organizing applications into some kind of logical framework. Code organization schemes are as old as computers. Back when computers used punch cards, programmers kept routines in tidy order. If you got a card out of sequence, your program did not function properly. And heaven forbid you drop a box of cards on the way to the computer—the result would be analogous to randomly reordering the lines in a CFML template!

The easiest concept to observe about Fusebox is the impact it has on an application's code--where files are stored how directories are arranged. The Fusebox specification defines how to arrange code into easy-to-manage chunks. When code is well organized, it is easy to read, explore, and maintain.

Although many people quickly recognize the value of using a standard approach to arranging code, some of the benefits are often overlooked.

ColdFusion has been a successful language primarily due to its low entry threshold. That is, ColdFusion does not require a great deal of study and knowledge of programming to get started.

Because so many people with no formal background in programming or application development get involved in developing ColdFusion applications, a great deal of ColdFusion code is disorganized or poorly written. Many developers are satisfied as long as the program delivers the expected result. This has caused ColdFusion's reputation to suffer unfairly. Instead of recognizing that ColdFusion accommodates an amazingly wide spectrum of experience from complete novice to application guru, rumor-mongers proclaimed that ColdFusion was a “toy language”, or that it could not scale well.

Scaling means that a completed application will be able to successfully handle workloads larger than those for which it was originally designed. In the case of web applications, it usually translates to a large increase in the number of page requests or simultaneous users that the system handles.

Database issues aside, when an application is poorly designed and constructed, it is generally not able to scale very well. Program logic that works well for one or two users might overstress the server when several hundred users all try to use it at once. Many ColdFusion applications are poorly designed and constructed, simply because their creators never considered the issues involved in effective application design.

However, ColdFusion's reputation as a small-scale application server is not deserved, and indeed has been greatly reduced in recent years. Projects such as RoomsToGo.com (the largest retailer of furniture online), MySpace.com (one of the highest traffic sites on the Internet) and the federal government's Section 508 (accessibility) compliance site have proven that CFML can scale effectively when the application is properly conceived and executed. All three of these high-volume sites are written in CFML, and all three also use Fusebox.

A Way to Manage Growing Applications

The responsibilities of a manager can be defined by a constant struggle to determine when a project will be completed and how much it will cost. If, as a manager, you do not have a good idea of how the application's code is organized, then the uncertainty factor rises rapidly. Fusebox project managers have a much easier job, due to the high degree of organization inherent to Fusebox applications. Additionally, the wealth of metadata captured in Fusebox's XML vocabularies provides a great deal of power for project management.

Using Fusebox is good for project managers, but Fusebox also mimics the way managers work. If you have ever managed a project, you know that most of your time is spent coordinating the efforts of others. Managers do not directly produce the end product; rather they encourage and enable those underneath them to produce more, better, faster. They are skilled at assigning tasks to appropriate resources, which helps manage a project's size. A comparison of Fusebox and corporate managers reveals that they share some of the same methods for getting work done. Fusebox encourages code to be highly specialized and focused. The structure helps to control all the smaller pieces. And Fusebox 5.5 adds a great deal of flexibility in terms of the structural design of the application.

If you are a reader of Scott Adams' *Dilbert* comic strip, you are quite familiar with the Pointy-Haired Boss (PHB), the epitome of a manager without a clue. Dilbert is funny because we can relate to the title character; most of us have worked for a PHB at one time or another, or known someone who has. Consequently, it might be hard to imagine corporate managers as a model for solving a problem, but there is a reason that management hierarchy rules the structure of companies today.

People can only process so much information in any given day. Using a flat organization (where managers are nonexistent and everyone is an equal), every member of the group must communicate his ideas and information to every other member of the group on a regular basis. Obviously, this is inefficient and can easily grow to the point where everyone spends all his time involved in communication, with no time left to actually get work done.

ColdFusion applications that lack a real structure act similarly. Every page can link to every other page. In fact, every page must link directly to each other page it knows about to get something done. If a new page is added, all the other pages that refer to it must be updated. There is a high degree of coupling between code templates—an indication of a fragile system.

This is where the manager comes in. Sacrifice one person's ability to directly produce but give that person the role of facilitating communication, and everyone else gets more done. By filtering out all the other stuff that goes around other parts of the organization, team members can focus on the skills for which they were hired in the first place.

The manager can see the "big picture" of the organization--what projects are currently underway, what areas of uncertainty lie ahead, and what teams need resources to complete their job. A good manager is a master delegator. If a manager goes "into the trenches" to produce and directly contribute, communication suffers and projects slow down.

PHBs notwithstanding, by organizing and regulating the flow of information between teams, managers streamline business. Fusebox duplicates the purpose of a manager by handling the interaction within the application. If an employee needs to arrange a meeting with another department to complete a project, the manager knows whom to contact and facilitates the communication. Similarly, if a web site user wants to see a list of all products on sale, the Fusebox controller knows which files accomplish that task. So instead of having links directly to other templates, a Fusebox template has links to the controller that just indicate what link was clicked, rather than which specific template to call. This results in a decoupled application which is much easier to maintain.

A Way to Think About Applications

When you sit down to work with an application, do you have a mental concept of it in your head? What does it look like in your mind's eye? Can you fit it all into your head at once? Do you think of the application's code as being organized in a particular way, or does it all just sort of run together in a big jumble?

Part of the problem of working with unorganized code is just trying to envision the application. Without a defined model, the picture that forms tends to be abstract. It is hard to imagine what happens when a particular template runs, how information is passed from one template to another, and what a change in one template does to another template. You might tend to think in terms of web servers and page requests or maybe streams of ones and zeros flying around if you understand that kind of thing. Although there is nothing wrong with this view, there is nothing tangible about it either. You cannot visualize the application. Or, as Beethoven said:

> "[The work] rises, it grows, I hear and see the image in front of me from every angle...and only the labor of writing it down remains..."

Beethoven was a musical genius who was fully capable of composing a complete symphony in his head. Most folks are not as good at programming as Beethoven was at composing; we need structure for our applications. Thankfully, we use things every day that can give us some valuable models for our applications. One example that closely resembles Fusebox is a computer network router.

Fusebox Mimics Networks

Over time, routers have helped organize network traffic immensely. Two of the most successful early network topologies were ring and bus architectures, shown in Illustration 1.

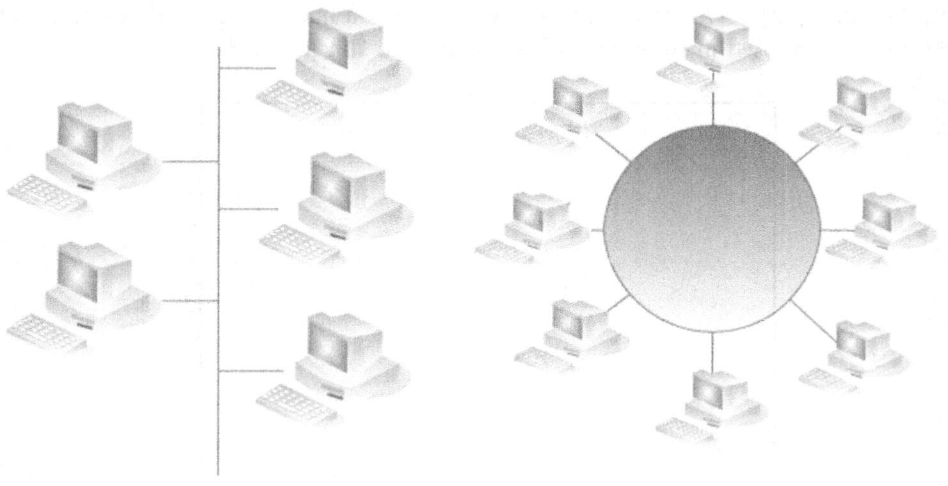

Illustration 1 - Bus and Ring Networks

These two architectures had one thing in common: They were based, as are all networks, on the idea of broadcasting packets of data from one machine to another.

As Illustration 1 shows, the bus architecture worked by machines sending packets addressed to other machines onto the bus, the central line in the figure. Each machine would check the address on every packet that went by. If the packet belonged to the machine, it would make a copy of the packet and read it. Otherwise, the packet would be ignored.

Acting somewhat like a bus network in a loop, IBM's Token Ring worked by each packet attaching a token that carried the address of the recipient. When the token passed the recipient machine, the machine stripped off the packet. If the token passed a non-recipient machine, nothing happened and it continued around the ring.

Both of these approaches meant that a lot of packets were flying around on the wires. Then came a new topology, and the problem got worse.

The newer topology, called a star, used a central hub to send packets from one machine to another. A hub was a simple concept; it took whatever came in one port and sent copies of it out on all the other ports. This made great sense when you had a single hub at the center of several computers. Shown in Illustration 2 is the classic star network.

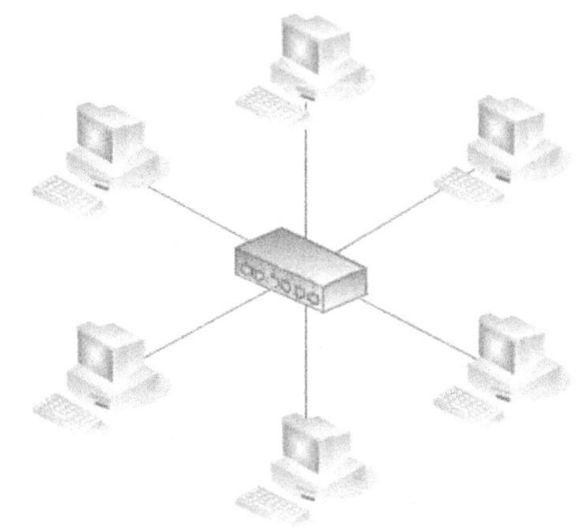

Illustration 2 - Star Network

Networks based on hubs eventually reached a practical limit on the number of ports, so network engineers expanded the capacity of the hub by linking hubs together. However, that technique was not scalable. Since each hub copied every incoming packet onto every outgoing port, the number of packets multiplied exponentially. If you linked too many hubs, the multiplied traffic would cause collision problems, with traffic moving slowly.

The answer to this problem was the router. A router is the hub's smarter cousin. Whereas a hub simply copies what is received in one port to all the other ports, a router sends a packet only to the destination port. Using strategically placed routers, network planners were able to create huge networks. In fact, the Internet is a series of interconnected routers.

By organizing and regulating the flow of traffic between workgroups, network routers streamlined the networking industry. Routers act as a big switch. If one computer wants to talk to another computer, the router essentially connects those two machines to each other. Similarly, Fusebox uses a master controller file to directly pipe a page request to the correct set of files. The controller file handles every action that the system can perform.

Nonstructured ColdFusion applications have no hub. Page requests are all point-to-point. As the system grows in size, developers can't remember which pages link where. It becomes extremely difficult to keep a clear picture of the application in your head. The classic illustration is a plate of spaghetti. Imagine trying to memorize exactly what a pile of spaghetti looks like and where each noodle winds. Fusebox eases the task of understanding the application's structure.

Back to Thinking About Applications

We started this discussion with the idea that applications are difficult to think about in tangible terms, and that Fusebox provides an easier concept to grasp. Each of the real-world examples (network routers and managers) is tangible if you are familiar with it. When someone mentions one of these examples, you instantly have an idea of what it is about and how it works.

Fusebox does something similar with applications. As you gain experience with Fusebox, you will become more comfortable with the associated terminology and your applications will be easier to visualize. So let's take a look at the principles embodied by Fusebox.

Technical Fusebox Principles

You are probably beginning to think, "Okay, enough with the metaphors. Just what makes a Fusebox application in the real world?" Fair enough. Fusebox has many technical aspects. Some people use all the ideas that have ever been labeled "Fusebox," whereas others only use some core components. For an application to be considered "Fusebox," it should exhibit the following characteristics:

1. Use the Fusebox method of file and directory organization.

2. Use the Fusebox core files.

3. Control the flow of the application using a "fuseaction".

4. Employ exit fuseactions (XFAs).

5. Use Fusedocs in all fuse files.

What happens if an application only uses some of the five characteristics? Usually its developers call it "a variation of Fusebox." It might work perfectly well in its own development environment, but it loses some of the benefits of using a common framework.

The power of a widely used framework and methodology is lost. Most industries standardize on a certain set of specifications. When that happens, the industry booms.

Throughout the book, we will look at other ideas and practices that (although not all Fusebox developers use them) are considered Fusebox "best practices." The next few sections provide some Fusebox basics so we can start to fit the whole picture together. Welcome to technical Fusebox.

File and Directory Organization

Any time an application has more than a few files, it makes sense to reorganize them into a set of folders. Imagine you start a new school semester with a new laptop computer and you stick all your schoolwork in My Documents. After the first week, you have ten files in there--a few Word documents, maybe an Excel spreadsheet of your class schedule, a mind map you created in Biology class, and a handful of text files of notes. By the next week, the number of files has doubled to 20. Sensing impending disaster by file overload, you wisely create folders for each of your classes and segregate your files. This works wonderfully through the end of the school year, but the next fall rolls around and you have all those folders from old classes--too many of them to quickly access folders for your current classes. You create a new folder called Freshman Year and move all your class folders from last year into that new folder. "Hey, I'm getting organized," you think. And you are right. Using folders to logically and physically separate files and subfolders is mandatory after you get more than a few of them together.

What's the difference between "logically" and “physically" separating files and folders? Determining that you had too many files and putting them into separate folders is the physical separation. However, you didn't just create folders called folder1, folder2, and folder3 and randomly stick files in each one until they were equally full. You carefully named your folders Biology 101, Intro to Java, and Cultural Anthropology and placed the files that you created for each of those classes into the corresponding folder. That is what is meant by "logically." Maybe your Intro to Java folder has twice as many files as Biology 101, but it makes sense to organize them according to class, not according to count.

The way we organize files and folders in Fusebox is nothing radical; it is just an extension of logical organization. Take, for instance, the site map of a couple HTML pages pictured in Illustration 3.

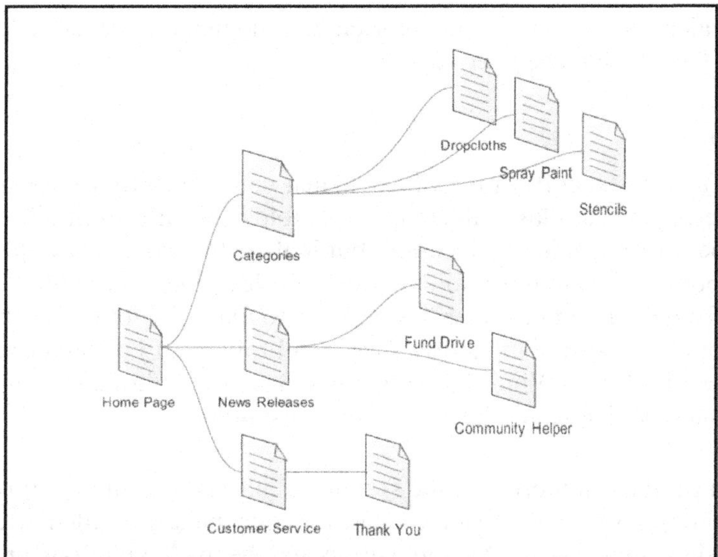

Illustration 3 - Simple HTML site map

The site map in Illustration 3 is an example of the directory structure shown in Illustration 4.

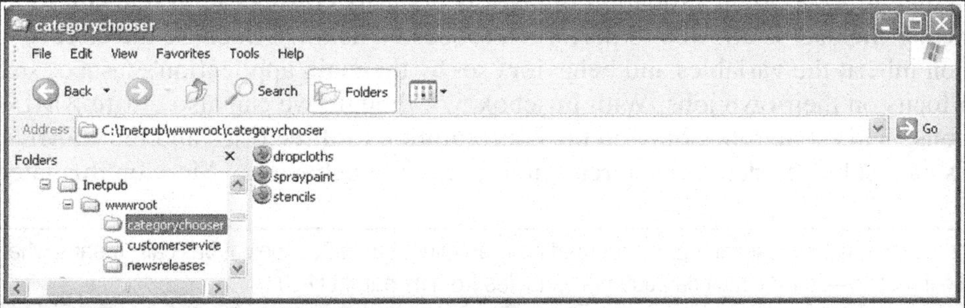

Illustration 4 - Simple HTML Site Directory Structure

If the web site shown in Illustration 4 were a Fusebox application, then the subfolders customerservice, newsreleases, and categorychooser would be called *circuits*. On the most basic level, a Fusebox circuit is just a directory. In Windows terminology, there are folders and subfolders, but in Fusebox, there is only one name for any directory, regardless of how deeply nested it is. Frequently, Fusebox developers refer to a circuit as being a *child* circuit of another circuit. That just means that a circuit is nested inside another circuit. Child circuits were prevalent in Fusebox 3, but are seen less in later versions, due to the more flexible nature of layouts in these later versions.

Circuit Inheritance

Circuits are more than just a collection of files. When you (using your imagination) organized your freshman year class folders into one folder, what benefit did it bring? It reduced the number of folders in one location, but it also allowed you to apply security (if you had some important files in those folders) to one folder and have subfolders inherit the security settings from their parent folder. If you were to mark the folder Freshman Year as read-only, you would not be able to modify files in subfolders of Freshman Year. Imagine if this feature were not built into Windows; you would have to go through each file and modify its properties by hand, which would be quite time-consuming.

Fusebox 5.5 has a similar but more flexible system of inheritance. In fact, it is much more powerful than Windows' version. Inside each circuit may be a file called fusebox.xml[1]. This file defines a Fusebox application. An application may be made up of one or more circuits. Variables set in fusebox.xml are available to the rest of the application. In addition, we can use fusebox.xml to assign plugins that will operate at various points in the fuseaction's process. This means that we can, for example, apply security logic to check whether a user is logged in through the use of a Login circuit defined by the main circuit's fusebox.xml file. Then every circuit can forgo login validation in favor of security consideration relevant to itself (e.g., whether the user is allowed to perform a requested action). Because the circuits in the application inherit the variables and behaviors set by the main application's fusebox.xml file, they can focus on their own jobs. With Fusebox 5.5, though, we can also create XML-less applications. This style relies only on the configuration of directories and the CFML templates themselves to determine circuit and fuseaction behaviors. More on this later.

Note: *Inheritance* is a term used in object-oriented programming, but in Fusebox, it basically means what it sounds like it means--a child circuit can use the variables from its parent circuit.

One good way to decide how to divide an application into circuits is to determine what parts of the application might be considered miniature applications, or logical collections of behavior. If we were building an e-commerce site , we might have circuits for catalog/product functions, product reviews, checkout, customer service, search and user

[1]The fusebox.xml file is only required if the circuit will be called directly as an application's main circuit and the XML-based approach to Fusebox is being used.

management. Let's not forget about the home circuit, too. Every application needs a home circuit, which is used to tie all the circuits together into one application.

There is no hard and fast set of rules for organizing circuits. A Fusebox application's circuits can be organized in whatever fashion makes sense to its architect. A large site might be a single large Fusebox application with many circuits, or it might a federation of several smaller Fusebox applications. These are decisions the architect makes.

File Organization

To review the terminology acquired thus far, a folder or directory in Fusebox is called a *circuit*. Any subfolders or subdirectories are said to be *child circuits* of the circuit above them, which might be called the *parent circuit*. There is also a distinction in the term for a file, which Fusebox calls a *fuse*. Often, ColdFusion files are called *templates*. Although the terms *template*, *file*, *page*, and *fuse* are relatively interchangeable, a file that is used as a fuse in a Fusebox application carries two unique distinctions that any old ColdFusion template or file does not necessarily have: structured naming conventions and rules of use.

Structured Naming Conventions

The first distinction is that Fusebox fuses follow a carefully defined yet extensible file-naming system. The content that can and should be contained in a fuse depends on its file prefix.

Fuse Prefix	Fuse Type	Description
dsp_	Display	Only fuse type that should contain display code, be it HTML, WML, SOAP packets, or something other form of display output.
qry_	Query	Only fuse type that should perform database interactions whether it be via <cfquery> or <cfstoredproc>. Always returns a recordset.
act_	Action	Any code that does not fall into the previous two fuse types. Used primarily for data manipulation, and external systems interaction such as <cfmail>, <cfpop>, and so on.

NOTE: Some Fuseboxers don't use the underscore between the fuse prefix and the rest of the name.

Table 1 - Fuse Prefixes

For the majority of files in a Fusebox application, exactly what code should get which of the preceding three fuse prefixes is a no-brainer. A fuse that runs a <cfquery> tag to get a recordset of all products in a database with prices over $30 would use the qry_ prefix (e.g., qry_GetProducts.cfm). A fuse that loops over a recordset created by a qry_ fuse and displays each row formatted into a <table> would use the dsp_ prefix (e.g., dsp_showProducts.cfm). A fuse that performs some complex validation based on the results of a user-submitted form would use the act_ fuse prefix (e.g., act_validateProduct.cfm).

In Fusebox 3, The fbx_ prefix was used for the reserved Fusebox framework files--those files that got the Fusebox job done by creating the inheritance structure, creating the central controller file, handling the layout and nesting of displays, and other tasks. These files are not longer used as of Fusebox 4. They have been replaced in Fusebox 5 by the fusebox5.cfm file and the application and circuit configuration files (fusebox.xml and circuit.xml). As previously noted, in Fusebox 5.5, these configuration files are optional, depending on the level of control you want over your application, and the type of application configuration desired.

The second distinction between a plain ColdFusion template and a Fusebox fuse is that each fuse should perform a discrete task. If a user is placing an order at the end of a checkout process, an example system has a number of tasks to perform including checking the inventory, verifying and processing the credit card, updating the inventory, inserting the order into the database, sending an email to the shipping and accounting departments, sending an email to the customer, and finally displaying a "thank you" page to the customer. Each one of these steps would be comprised of one or more fuses. A good Fusebox developer would not combine these steps into one fuse, as tempting as it might be. A good rule of thumb is that most query and action fuses should fit on one screen in your favorite editor. While there are necessary exceptions to this rule, it's a good guide to keep in mind.

Fuse Rules of Use

Here are a few rules to keep in mind about what kind of code should and should not be in contained within certain fuse types.

For action fuses that use the act_ prefix, there is no display code. Whether the requesting client is a browser, a web service, or a <cfmodule> tag, act_ fuses can only contain CFML logic and service calls. Use of <cfoutput> should be strictly limited to looping over query recordsets to perform manipulations of the data, and it is more usual to use <cfloop> for this purpose. In rare instances, an action fuse can perform database queries if, for example, you are trying to emulate the functionality of a stored procedure by running a query, looping through it, and performing subsequent queries based on the results of the first query. However, it would be wisest to <cfinclude> that nested query as a qry_ fuse. Here is an example of an action fuse that creates a name list:

```
<!--- act_nameBuild.cfm --->
<cfset nameList="">
<cfloop collection="#attributes.stName#" item="aName">
<cfset nameList=ListAppend(nameList,aName,)>
</cfloop>
```

This code takes a structure of names (attributes.stName) and creates a list of the key values (nameList).

Like action fuses, query fuses that use the qry_ prefix cannot present display to the client. Query fuses should be as modular as possible to allow maximum reuse of the query. This means that the only code that should be contained in a qry_ fuse is the <cfquery> (or <cfstoredproc>) tag, a few <cfparam> tags to create defaults for the query, and maybe some looping afterward to rearrange the data output if it could not be accomplished in the query. Query fuses must always generate a recordset. It is also a good idea to name the recordset (via the name attribute in the <cfquery> tag) the same name as the fuse, minus the file extension and fuse prefix. For example, the fuse qry_customerDetails.cfm has a recordset called customerDetails:

```
<!--- qry_customerDetails.cfm --->
<cfparam name="attributes.customerID" default="">
<cfquery name=" customerDetails" datasource="#request.dsn#">
 SELECT *
  FROM customerDetails
 WHERE customerID=#attributes.customerID#
</cfquery>
```

Unlike the previous two fuses, display fuses are the only type that can present output to the client. As a consequence, display fuses should contain a minimal amount of ColdFusion logic. Common ColdFusion tags that are used in display fuses include <cfoutput>, <cfloop>, <cfset>, <cfparam>, and <cfif>. Of course, you are free to use whatever tags are necessary to get the job done for a fuse, but if you find yourself writing blocks of ColdFusion code, it should probably be moved into an action fuse. Here is an example of a display fuse:

```
<!--- dsp_customerDetails.cfm --->
<table border="1">
 <tr>
  <td>Name</td>
  <td>Managers</td>
 </tr>
<cfoutput>
 <tr>
  <td>#customerDetails.name#</td>
  <td>#nameList#</td>
 </tr>
</cfoutput>
</table>
```

Because Fusebox encourages different kinds of code to be created in different fuse types, the result is a complete separation of display from business logic. Due to this separation, debugging is easier, team coding is simplified, development is faster, and the entire application exhibits increased cohesion.

Note: *Cohesion* relates how well a fuse, fuseaction, or circuit performs exactly one function or achieves a single goal.

The Fusebox Evolution

Applications that were developed in early versions of Fusebox (pre-FB3) consisted of a "federation" of circuits; in a metaphysical sense, each circuit lived in its own world, only vaguely aware of ties to other circuits. Circuits did not share the benefits of inheritance. To simulate inheritance, it was commonplace to tie circuits together, which reduced modularity. Extended Fusebox (XFB), created by Hal Helms, was developed to solve these problems. XFB gave circuits complete independence from each other but also created a true structure among the circuits, uniting them into one "wrapper" application. Fusebox 3 built on XFB by using a formalized set of core files that set up a structure for the circuits, created a system of inheritance and settings, provided for the switch-case that controls the application flow, and controlled layouts and nested displays. Each core file used the fbx_ prefix.

While all this structure was useful, it was also a bit constraining. Inheritance of layout components as well as variables relied on the circuit hierarchy of the application. This was a powerful concept when we were considering applications of circuits arranged in multi-tiered hierarchies. But reality soon set in: we discovered that the vast majority of Fusebox applications were designed as two-tier hierarchies, and the requirements of the FB3 core files were dictating the location of circuits within the application. The tail had come to wag the dog.

Fusebox 4 adopted a much more flexible approach to the application hierarchy, allowing circuits to participate in the application in various places regardless of their placement within the filesystem hierarchy. In order to achieve this flexibility, the core was completely redesigned and the core files replaced. Fusebox 5 retains the functionality of Fusebox 4, but uses a different set of core files. Fusebox 5.5 maintains the functionality of Fusebox 5, but adds the ability to create XML-less applications that “feel” more like the earlier philosophy of Fusebox.

In fact, Fusebox 5.5 was initiated in response to two philosophical design goals:

> 1. Simplify. Remove barriers. Make it easier for newbies. Make building applications faster by favoring convention over configuration.
>
> 2. Extend through extensibility. Provide new functionality outside the core. Add plugins, lexicons, even standardized circuits.[1]

Thanks to this carefully considered direction, Fusebox 5.5 allows us to work in a variety of ways while still honoring the basic philosophies of Fusebox.

These two themes will reappear throughout this book, as we look at the techniques that are available in Fusebox 5.5. Whenever possible, we'll compare the various ways to approach a given problem. This will allow us to choose the techniques that best fit with our own preferred methods, as well as giving us other approaches to consider as we build new applications.

[1]From releasenotes.pdf for Fusebox 5.5.

Controlling the Flow

Controlling program flow is an essential aspect of Fusebox. To see why, let's take a few minutes for an off-topic discussion.

Do you ever find yourself flying more than you would like? I fly commercially a few times a year, and out of all the frequent-flyer miles I've accumulated, very few were on delayed flights. I've seldom been "bumped," and for the most part, the tickets were inexpensive and I was able to get on the flights I wanted, even on short notice. Even in post-9/11 America.

But if this were 1950, it's unlikely I would have had such success. Back then, airlines were frequently late, ticket prices were higher, and direct flights were the only way you could fly. If you wanted to go from Los Angeles to New Orleans, you had to wait for a long time for a direct flight, or take any number of intermediate flights, each one quite expensive, and there was little guarantee that you would not miss a connecting flight. Airlines were operating on a point-to-point system but recognized that something needed to change to allow an increase in cities served, passenger volume, and profits realized. In the early 1960s, United Airlines created the world's first hub-and-spoke system of airports, linking western U.S. routes with eastern U.S. routes via major connecting hubs. At the time, the other major airlines were nay-saying this model, claiming it would destroy the industry. However, after a few short years, all the airlines had their own hub-and-spoke systems.

The system used by the airline industry today is similar to the system used by Fusebox. In addition, the system used by the airline industry up until the early 1960s is similar to most non-Fusebox ColdFusion applications. Non-Fusebox ColdFusion applications tend to rely on direct page-to-page links. A form that is collecting information submits to a form-processing page. The form-processing page in turn links to a "thank you" page. In Fusebox applications, every page links to a single controller file, which then processes the user's request. If you are on a page with a form, it submits to the Fusebox, which then passes control to the form-processing page. The links, form actions, Javascript redirects, `<cfmodule>`, and `<cflocation>` tags are the spokes that go through the Fusebox hub.

Illustration 5 shows a comparison of point-to-point versus hub-and-spoke systems in airlines and web applications. Point-to-point models can work well in small sizes, but they must be upgraded to hub-and-spoke systems to handle increases in traffic and complexity.

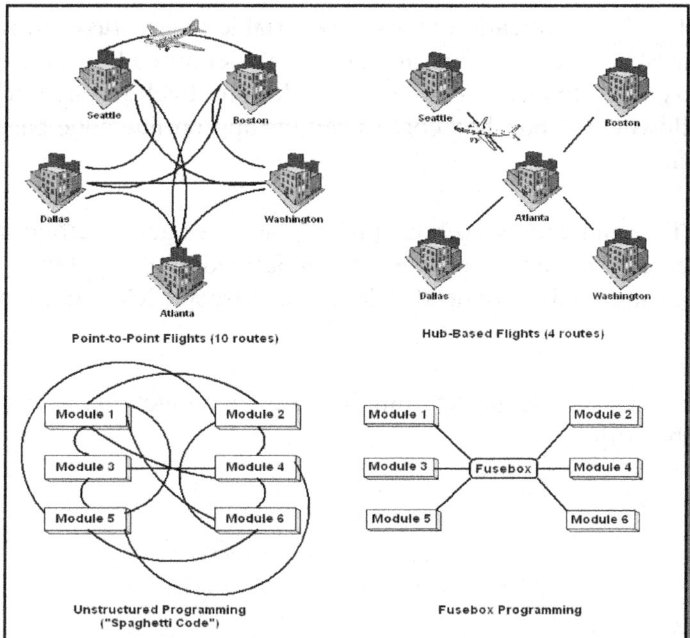

Illustration 5 - Point-to-Point vs. Hub-and-Spoke

A Look at Circuits and Fuseactions

So what makes a Fusebox application able to process in this hub-based fashion? In ColdFusion, the browser requests a .cfm template, and the web server picks up the request and passes it off to the ColdFusion Application Server. From there, ColdFusion processes the page, including any additional files needed (e.g., <cfinclude>s). When ColdFusion is done, the finished HTML page goes back to the web server and the web server returns it to the browser. But in Fusebox, instead of pointing to individual templates, the browser always points to one file: the default web document, which is usually index.cfm.

This index.cfm file includes the core file (fusebox5.cfm), which runs code to set up the Fusebox framework and process the request, including fuses from the circuits as necessary. But again, how does Fusebox know what fuses are required if the request always goes to index.cfm?

Every request in a Fusebox application includes a variable named **fuseaction**[1]. This variable's value consists of a circuit alias and an action, delimited by a dot. This is all the information Fusebox needs to know what code should run. Each fuseaction is defined in the specified circuit, allowing the Fusebox core to call the appropriate code based on the specified fuseaction.

In typical modern (FB4 and later) Fusebox apps, all the fuses get specified in the circuit.xml file for the requested circuit, and the circuits are all defined in the application's fusebox.xml file. The use of XML means that we need to learn the Fusebox XML vocabulary, but that's not a major hurdle.

Here is an example circuit.xml file, taken from the “Wegot Widgets” (Basic) reference application at Fusebox.org:

```
<circuit access="public">
  <fuseaction name="showCatalog">
    <xfa name="lnkProductName" value="browse.showProduct" />
    <xfa name="lnkAdmin" value="Admin.showNewProductForm" />
    <include template="qryGetCatalog" />
    <include template="dspCatalog"/>
  </fuseaction>

  <fuseaction name="showProduct">
   <xfa name="lnkBackToCatalog" value="browse.showCatalog" />
   <include template="qryGetProduct" />
    <include template="dspProduct" />
  </fuseaction>
</circuit>
```

Notice in particular the first section surrounded by the <fuseaction> tags. This section specifies a fuseaction named showWelcome. It requires two templates named qryGetCatalog and dspDatalog. Wait! There's no file extension on either of these file names. This is one illustration of the platform-independence of Fusebox 4/5. The Fusebox core worries about the file extension, adding “.cfm” in the ColdFusion environment, or “.php” if we're working in PHP.

That is all there is to a circuit.xml file. We will do a little more explaining later, but for now, just think of the Fusebox as a big switchboard, running different code depending on a user-supplied variable. The variable can actually be named as we choose, but the default is “fuseaction”.

[1]The fuseaction variable can be renamed; for clarity we'll always call it *fuseaction*.

Fuseactions Control Flow

Whatever its name, the fuseaction variable controls the flow of the application. That is, it tells the Fusebox core what to do next. In order to do this successfully, the value of the fuseaction variable must include both the name of a circuit and the name of a fuseaction within that circuit. For example, to run the "welcome" fuseaction in the "main" circuit, any of the requests shown below will satisfy this requirement. Fusebox selects the appropriate action based on the variable fuseaction, which is passed on the URL string like this:

```
<a href="index.cfm?fuseaction=main.welcome">
```

or in a hidden form field like this:

```
<input type="Hidden" name="fuseaction" value="main.welcome">
```

or in a <cflocation> tag like this:

```
<cflocation url="index.cfm?fuseaction=main.welcome">
```

or in a <cfmodule> tag like this:

```
<cfmodule template="index.cfm" fuseaction="main.welcome">
```

Every time index.cfm (or whatever the default web document is named) is run, it expects the variable fuseaction to be passed in. However, sometimes that variable is not passed in. This case occurs when a user types in something like this:

```
http://www.fusebox.org/
```

There is no ?fuseaction=main.welcome in that URL, so Fusebox needs a default fuseaction. Default fuseactions are key to understanding how a Fusebox application responds. The default fuseaction is typically set in the parameters section of the home circuit's fusebox.xml file. Here's a sample parameters block from a fusebox.xml file; look for the defaultfuseaction definition in the third line.

```
<parameters>
    <parameter name="fuseactionVariable" value="fuseaction" />
    <parameter name="defaultFuseaction" value="main.welcome" />
    <parameter name="precedenceFormOrUrl" value="form"/>
    <parameter name="mode" value="development"/>
    <parameter name="password" value=""/>
    <parameter name="parseWithComments" value="true" />
    <parameter name="conditionalParse" value="false" />
    <parameter name="ignoreBadGrammar" value="false"/>
    <parameter name="useAssertions" value="true" />
    <parameter name="scriptlanguage" value="cfmx" />
    <parameter name="scriptFileDelimiter" value="cfm"/>
    <parameter name="maskedFileDelimiters" value="htm,cfm,cfml,php,php4,asp,aspx"/>
    <parameter name="characterEncoding" value="utf-8"/>
</parameters>
```

Now for every request of the Fusebox application, we can be assured that a fuseaction is available, even if one isn't specified in the request. The system can respond appropriately. With the fuseaction defined, the framework knows which fuseaction to run, and which circuit owns that fuseaction.

Since Fusebox 5.5 also allows XML-less configurations, we need a way to specify a default fuseaction without using fusebox.xml. All we need to do is set the value of the FUSEBOX_PARAMETERS.defaultFuseaction variable.

```
<cfset FUSEBOX_PARAMETERS.defaultFuseaction = "main.welcome" />
```

We can set the FUSEBOX_PARAMETERS.defaultFuseaction variable anywhere in the Fusebox request cycle before the actual call to the fuseaction takes place. This generally means one of three places: index.cfm, application.cfm, or fusebox.application.init.cfm.

Which Circuit Runs?

As we saw above, the fuseaction variable always contains two values in what we refer to as a *compound fuseaction*. We know that the second part of the fuseaction is the action; it determines which set of fuses is run for a given user request. Imagine that a user requests the **order.basket** fuseaction like this:

```
<form action="index.cfm?fuseaction=order.basket" method="post">
```

We know that the **basket** fuseaction will be run, but we also know that the **order** circuit should handle the request for that fuseaction. Using this compound fuseaction, we can specify any fuseaction in any circuit to be run. The first part is always the circuit, and the second part is always the fuseaction.

Imagine that a customer is buying a product on an e-commerce site. Halfway through the checkout process, she decides to review the company's privacy policy. All of the fuses in the checkout process are in a circuit named **checkout**. The page that she wants to see, **dsp_privacy.cfm**, is in a fuseaction named **privacy** in the **policy** circuit. We would write the link from the checkout page to the privacy policy like this:

```
<a href="index.cfm?fuseaction=policy.privacy">
```

The first file that runs is index.cfm, which is the file that the link requested. The Fusebox calling file (fusebox5.cfm) is included from the index.cfm page[1]. The Fusebox core establishes the framework and calls the circuit.xml file from the **policy** circuit, which has a <fuseaction> block that looks like this:

```
<fuseaction name="privacy">
  <include template="dsp_privacy">
</fuseaction>
```

The dsp_privacy.cfm file is processed because the second part of the fuseaction (the part after the dot) matches the <fuseaction name="privacy"> tag. After Fusebox finishes processing, the display file is presented to the customer, who is satisfied with the privacy of your site and happily completes her purchase.

The process works the same way for XML-less applications; the only difference is in the way the circuits and fuseactions are defined. We'll look at these approaches in more detail in later chapters. @@@[Left off here]

Exit Fuseactions

Each fuse is specialized and knows its job well ("I insert a new customer into the database." "I display the privacy policy," and so on). But because each fuse may contain links, form actions, and <cflocation>s, each fuse must know where those links go--what the circuits are called and what fuseactions are in which circuits. But this is not appropriate information to put in each fuse. Fuses should be designed so that they contain as few dependencies on (that is, knowledge of) the rest of the application as possible. We use Exit Fuseactions (XFAs) rather than hard-coded fuseactions within fuses as a means to reduce dependencies. An Exit Fuseaction is just a fuseaction stored in a variable. Here is a sample XFA from a display fuse that uses a form:

[1]We are temporarily ignoring the use of a variable such as self or myself to store the name of index.cfm-equivalent file. Such use is common practice in Fusebox, though.

```
<form action="index.cfm?fuseaction=#xfa.submit#" method="post">
```

XFA values are set in circuit.xml just before the fuse <include> directives:

```
<fuseaction name="privacy">
  <xfa name="continueLink" value="policy.payments">
  <xfa.name="backLink" value="policy.security">
  <include template="dsp_privacy">
</fuseaction>
```

This allows the circuit.xml file to control where each fuse it calls is allowed to go next. In the preceding case, the file dsp_privacy.cfm has two links: a "continue" and a "back" to guide an inquisitive customer through the array of site policies. The XFA names continueLink and backLink indicate both the job and the type of exit—in this case both are links. Other XFAs might have names like searchButton, itemImage or updateSuccess.

In XML-less applications, XFAs are set in CFML instead of XML, but they are still typically set just before including the fuse file in which the exit exists. To perform the fuseaction seen above in a CFM-based XML-less app, we might see the following code inside the **privacy.cfm** fuseaction file:

```
<cfset xfa.continueLink = "policy.payments">
<cfset xfa.backLink = "policy.security">
<cfinclude template="dsp_privacy.cfm">
```

Each fuse should not be required to be aware of its surroundings, so its own exit locations must be dynamic. This becomes especially important if a fuse links to another circuit. If the target circuit is moved or no longer exists, the fuse does not need to be updated--only the circuit.xml file does. XFAs also promote reusability of code. By using XFAs, we can write the fuse once but use it in different locations, and the links can go to different places.

Finding Out More

In this chapter, we've looked at some of the basic tenets of Fusebox and how it handles requests within a web application. We've seen how circuits work, how files are named and organized, circuits and fuseactions, and using Exit Fuseactions to reduce dependencies. These concepts represent a good start on Fusebox, but the discussion is in no way complete.

This book is intended to be a reference for building Fusebox 5.5 applications and the various approaches we have available for doing so. It is not a complete reference on Fusebox or the Fusebox Lifecycle Process (FLiP). For more information on those topics, you might want to take a look at *Fusebox 5 & FLiP: Master-Class ColdFusion Applications*, from Proton Arts.

So now let's get into the good stuff: a look at a “traditional” modern Fusebox application, followed by the same application executed using the approaches now available in Fusebox 5.5. It's time to drive!

Chapter 3 – "Traditional" Modern Fusebox

This chapter begins our examination of specific implementations of Fusebox 5.5. We're going to start by taking a look at a basic application that is implemented using "traditional" modern Fusebox. This terms sounds a bit self-contradictory, but it makes sense if we peel it apart a bit. By "modern Fusebox", we mean Fusebox 4 and later—the versions that support application and circuit configuration using XML files. We're using the term "traditional" to mean the way modern Fusebox apps were configured prior to Fusebox 5.5. That is, with XML files. Once we get a good look at this approach, we'll look at the pieces that have changed as of Fusebox 5.5, and then we'll look at the same application configured in the various ways that are available to us now.

Wegot Widgets Explained

To do all this comparing, we need an application that does more than a simple "Hello, World", but is also brief enough to be examined in-depth within the pages of this book. There is an application that was designed for just this purpose. It's called Wegot Widgets—the Fusebox reference application.

A reference application is nothing more than an application whose purpose is to support discussion of the concepts it uses. Wegot Widgets is a fictitious retail company, and variants of it web application can be found on fusebox.org. Let's take a look at what the application does.

Upon first visiting the site, the user is shown a list of all the widgets available from Wegot Widgets, as shown in Illustration 6.

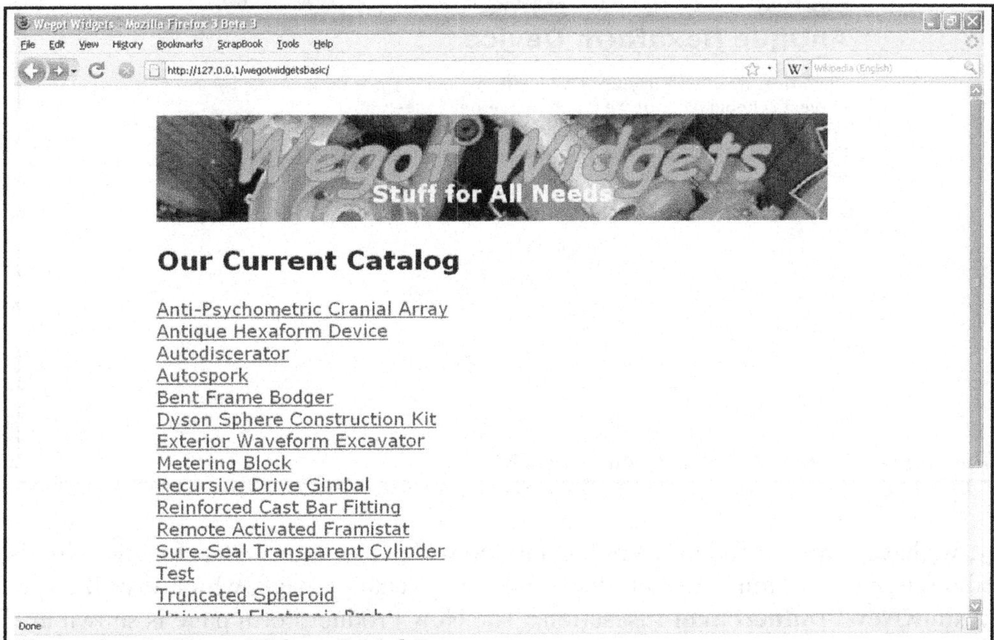

Illustration 6: Wegot Widgets Initial Page

When the user clicks on the name of any widget, a page with that widget's details is displayed. This is the **browse.showProduct** fuseaction, as shown in Illustration 7. The Back to Catalog link just goes back to the default page.

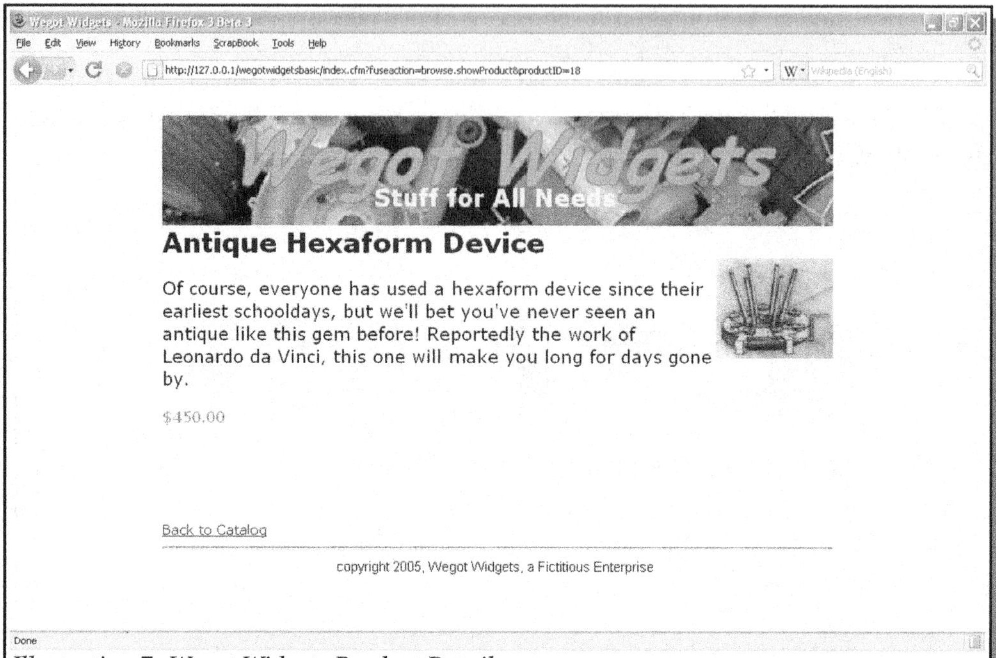

Illustration 7: Wegot Widgets Product Details

Finally, we have a way to add new products to the widgets catalog. That functionality is reached through the Admin - Add Products link on the catalog page, which fires the **Admin.showNewProductForm** fuseaction. The New Product Form page is shown in Illustration 8.

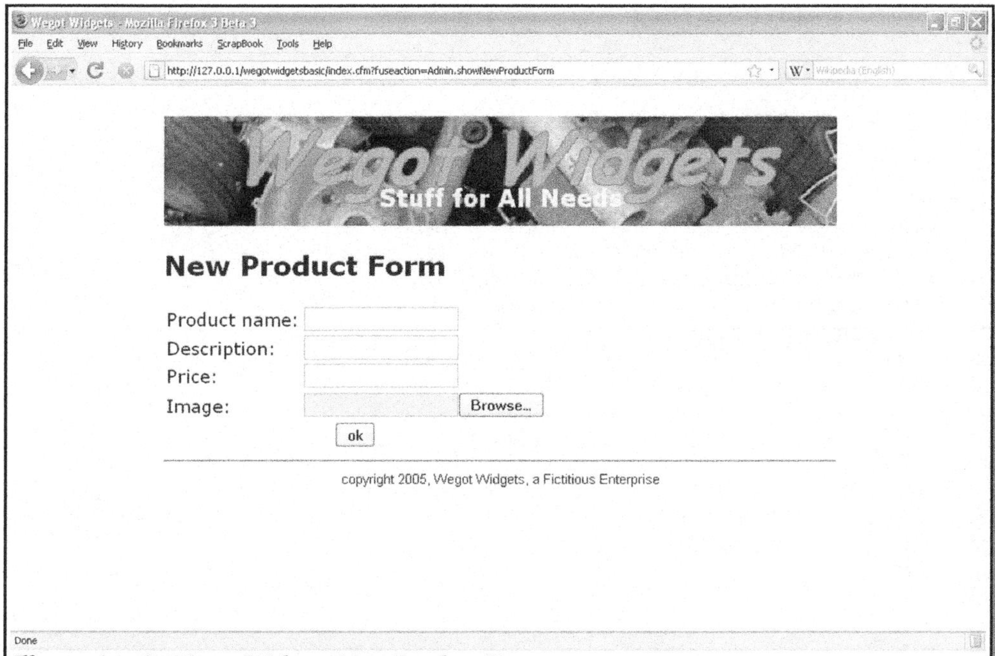

Illustration 8: Wegot Widgets New Product Form

Having taken a look at the functionality of the Wegot Widgets application, we can look at how the configuration of this version works. In subsequent chapters, we'll look at implementing the same functionality using the other approaches available in Fusebox 5.5.

Application Configuration

As a traditional modern Fusebox application, the Wegots Widgets basic implementation uses the fusebox.xml file for application configuration. The elements are fairly self-explanatory, so we won't take a lot of time to examine them, but we'll take a quick look at the entire file just so we'll have a baseline to compare the other approaches to application configuration in future chapters. Here's the fusebox.xml file for Wegot Widgets (basic):

```
<?xml version="1.0" encoding="UTF-8"?>
<fusebox>
  <circuits>
    <circuit alias="admin" path="admin/" />
    <circuit alias="browse" path="browse/" />
    <circuit alias="catalog" path="" />
  </circuits>
  <parameters>
    <parameter name="fuseactionVariable" value="fuseaction" />
    <parameter name="defaultFuseaction" value="browse.showCatalog" />
    <parameter name="precedenceFormOrUrl" value="form"/>
    <parameter name="mode" value="development"/>
    <parameter name="password" value=""/>
    <parameter name="parseWithComments" value="true" />
    <parameter name="conditionalParse" value="false" />
    <parameter name="ignoreBadGrammar" value="false"/>
    <parameter name="useAssertions" value="true" />
    <parameter name="scriptlanguage" value="cfmx" />
    <parameter name="scriptFileDelimiter" value="cfm"/>
    <parameter name="maskedFileDelimiters" value="htm,cfm,cfml,php,php4,asp,aspx"/>
    <parameter name="characterEncoding" value="utf-8"/>
  </parameters>
  <globalfuseactions>
    <appinit>
    </appinit>
    <preprocess>
      <do action="catalog.header" />
    </preprocess>
    <postprocess>
      <do action="catalog.footer" />
    </postprocess>
  </globalfuseactions>
  <plugins>
    <phase name="preProcess"></phase>
    <phase name="preFuseaction"></phase>
    <phase name="postFuseaction"></phase>
    <phase name="fuseactionException"></phase>
    <phase name="postProcess"></phase>
    <phase name="processError"></phase>
  </plugins>
</fusebox>
```

The application's configuration is defined by the various sections of this XML. In the next few pages, we'll take a look at these sections and how they contribute to the application's configuration. We trying to establish a baseline from which to compare other approaches. For more details on the fusebox.xml file, see *Fusebox 5 & FLiP: Master-Class ColdFusion Applications* (Proton Arts, 2007).

Default Fuseaction

One of the key things a Fusebox app needs to know is the default fuseaction. That is, which fuseaction to run if no fuseaction is specified. In the traditional modern model, this is accomplished with a parameter having a name attribute of **defaultFuseaction**. The value attribute of this element defines the default fuseaction. For the WegotWidgets application, this value is **browse.showCatalog**.

Parameters

Just as we set the default fuseaction using a parameter in the fusebox.xml file, we can set other parameters in similar fashion. Though our purpose is not to have an in-depth discussion of all these parameters, there are some changes to parameter behavior for Fusebox 5.5 that we should note.

Parameters for Parsing

The end result of a page request in a traditional modern Fusebox application is a parsed fuseaction file. This file is just a CFML template that contains all the code assembled by the requested fuseaction. Parsed fuseaction files are located in the **/parsed** directory.

How and when a fuseaction gets parsed are controlled by parameters in fusebox.xml. These parameters work in conjunction with one another, so they get a section all their own here. We'll start by looking at the mode parameter.

Parameter: mode

This parameter controls Fusebox's execution mode. The parsing of fuseaction files depends on the execution mode, as the following table shows:

Mode Parameter Value	Result
development-circuit-load	Parses the circuit.xmls as required for the requested fuseaction. Does not parse fusebox.xml or reinitialize the Fusebox framework. This mode is thread-safe, so it is a good choice to use when developing AJAX applications.
development-full-load	Parses fusebox.xml, reinitializes the Fusebox framework, and parses circuit.xmls as required for the requested fuseaction.
production	Parses XML files only if they are newer than the ones held in memory. Does not parse changed fuseactions.

Parameter: conditionalParse

This parameter controlled conditional parsing of fuseactions in Fusebox 4.x. It is ignored in Fusebox 5.x

Parameter: parsePath

This parameter allows the specification of a directory where parsed fuseaction files are generated. Relatives path are relative to the application directory; absolute paths (starting with / or \) are relative to the web root directory.

Other Parameters

Here are some other parameters whose treatment have changed in Fusebox 5. While these are not specific to version 5.5, the changes are note-worthy.

Parameter: scriptLanguage

This parameter is ignored in Fusebox 5.x.

Parameter: useAssertions

This parameter is ignored in Fusebox 5.x.

Parameter: ignoreBadGrammar

This parameter is ignored in Fusebox 5.x.

Parameter: allowLexicon

This parameter is ignored in Fusebox 5.x. Lexicons are inherently supported in FB5.

So the parameters section of the fusebox.xml file gives us a great deal of selective control over the application's behavior. The next section we'll look at is the circuits section.

Circuits Definition

One of the hallmarks of a Fusebox application is the way its behaviors are organized into circuits, or logical collections of behavior. The circuits section of fusebox.xml defines the circuits that are to be recognized as part of the application, where they are located, and the aliases by which they are known.

Nothing here has changed since Fusebox 5.1.

Global Fuseactions

Global fuseactions can be defined to run as part of every fuseaction. They are defined in terms of where in the Fusebox request cycle they are to be run: appinit, preprocess, or postprocess.

If fuseactions are defined within an appinit section, they will be run before Fusebox initializes the application. This means plugins are not available for appinit fuseactions.

The other two global sections, preprocess and postprocess, simply run the specified fuseaction(s) before and after, respectively, the requested fuseaction.

Initialization

With a traditional modern Fusebox application, the application framework is initialized by parsing the XML files and generating CFML templates for each specified fuseaction. This initialization is controlled by the mode parameter in fusebox.xml and the fusebox.load variable, as we saw in the preceding sections.

Although this is a basic point for Fusebox 4.x and 5.1 users, it is important to note for Fusebox 5.5, as the means of initializing the application changes when we take non-traditional approaches to the application architecture. We'll see these different approaches in the coming chapters.

So we've finished a quick tour of issues relating to fusebox.xml. Now we'll have a quick look at the circuit.xml, the circuit definition file.

Circuit Configuration

The circuit configuration file simply defines what happens when a fuseaction is called. Since a circuit is defined as a collection of fuseactions, it makes sense that the circuit configuration would define that collection.

Fuseaction Definition

As with Fusebox 4-5.1, when using the traditional modern approach to Fusebox 5.5, we define fuseactions in circuit.xml. Each fuseaction has a **fuseaction** element, which specifies the fuseaction's name, and contains within it **include** elements to specify which fuses the fuseaction contains. A fuseaction may also call fuseactions from other circuits using the **do** element.

Here's a sample circuit.xml file from the WegotWidgets (basic) application. The fuseaction definitions are very straightforward.

```
<circuit access="public">
  <fuseaction name="showCatalog">
    <xfa name="lnkProductName" value="browse.showProduct" />
    <xfa name="lnkAdmin" value="Admin.showNewProductForm" />
    <include template="qryGetCatalog" />
    <include template="dspCatalog"/>
  </fuseaction>

  <fuseaction name="showProduct">
    <xfa name="lnkBackToCatalog" value="browse.showCatalog" />
    <include template="qryGetProduct" />
    <include template="dspProduct" />
  </fuseaction>
</circuit>
```

As we look at other approaches to defining a Fusebox 5.5 application, we'll see that circuit.xml isn't the only way available to define fuseactions.

Summary

In this chapter, we've seen how the traditional modern approach to Fusebox handles application configuration, initialization, and circuit configuration. We also introduced the WegotWidgets reference application. In the coming chapters, we'll take a look at how the sample application can be approached in different ways using Fusebox 5.5.

Chapter 4 – Going XML-less

The first, and perhaps biggest, difference between Fusebox 5.5 and previous modern Fusebox versions is the ability to take advantage of the modern Fusebox framework without using XML configuration files for the application and circuit.

This chapter will cover the issues involved with discarding the Fusebox XML configuration files, and how Fusebox 5.5 enables us to do so. In later chapters we'll see complete examples of these approaches in action.

Factor 1: Fusebox Parameters

Chapter 3 showed us the traditional modern approach to setting parameters for a Fusebox application: the <parameters> section of fusebox.xml. But if we are to go XML-less, we clearly can't rely on that approach for setting parameters. We need something new. That "something" is the FUSEBOX_PARAMETERS structure.

The FUSEBOX_PARAMETERS structure does just as its name implies—it stores the values that, in the traditional modern Fusebox app, are found in the parameters section of fusebox.xml. The structure can be referenced (e.g., values can be set or retrieved) at any point after initialization of the Fusebox framework.

Illustration 9 shows a sample of the FUSEBOX_PARAMETERS structure for the WegotWidgets application. Note that we only need to set parameters that don't have default values, or have default values we want to overwrite.

struct	
ALLOWIMPLICITFUSEBOX	true
CONDITIONALPARSE	true
DEBUG	true
DEFAULTFUSEACTION	browse.showCatalog
ERRORTEMPLATESPATH	/fusebox5/errortemplates/
MODE	development-full-load
PASSWORD	[empty string]
STRICTMODE	true

Illustration 9: FUSEBOX_PARAMETERS Structure

We can choose to create the FUSEBOX_PARAMETERS structure in a couple of different places, depending on preference, local conventions, and/or the version of CFML server we're using. The most common places for this task is in either index.cfm, Application.cfm or Application.cfc.

Since Fusebox applications always call the main template, we can put the code for FUSEBOX_PARAMETERS in index.cfm (or whatever you've chosen for your main template). This works, but generally the preference for earlier versions of CFML servers is to use Application.cfm. Either way, the goal is to create the structure before the Fusebox core is called.

For CFML servers that support Application.cfc, this is the preferred place to put the code to create the FUSEBOX_PARAMETERS structure. Place the code inside the <cffunction> definition for the OnRequestStart function.

Regardless of which approach we chose, creating the FUSEBOX_PARAMETERS structure is the first step toward replacing the functionality found in the fusebox.xml configuration file. The next section looks through the rest of the file with an eye toward replacement.

Factor 2: Omitting fusebox.xml

While Fusebox 4 introduced a great deal of flexibility and power through the use of XML configuration files, there has been a sizable portion of the Fusebox community that felt burdened by the need to learn XML just to build Fusebox apps with the latest version. Many CFML developers got into development in part as a result of the low threshold of entry offered by the language. Consequently, one of the goals that was set for version 5.5 was the ability to work without XML at all, but retaining the benefits of the modern Fusebox framework. The first of the XML files to be removed is the application configuration file, fusebox.xml.

We've already looked at how to replace the <parameters> section of fusebox.xml, so now we just need to look at the remaining sections to see how we can get the same results without XML.

Circuits

The <circuits> section of fusebox.xml is perhaps the easiest to replace when using Fusebox 5.5. We can take a couple of different approaches, depending on whether we wish to use ColdFusion Components (CFCs) or not.

If we choose to use CFCs for our circuits, we just create a CFC with the name of each circuit. Each circuit CFC contains functions that have the names of each fuseaction within the circuit. The fuse files remain unchanged. The nice thing is that Fusebox goes looking for circuit CFCs in a logical hierarchy of locations, as shown in this list:

controller/*alias*.cfc
model/*alias*.cfc
view/*alias*.cfc

As implied by these locations, the use of CFCs to represent circuits is designed to support the implementation of an explicit Model-View-Controller design pattern.

If we don't want to use CFCs, all we need to do is create a circuit directory named for each circuit in the application. When getting a request, Fusebox will look for a directory with the circuit name. Once it finds the directory, Fusebox looks for a CFML template with the name of the fuseaction. That template contains all the usual CFML code we would find in a fuseaction section of the fbx_switch file in a pre-4.0 Fusebox application.

A circuit-named directory may also contain CFCs to represent fuseactions, instead of a regular CFML template. If a CFC is used to represent a fuseaction, it contains only one function, named **do**. This function contains the CFML code as it would be found in a CFML template for the same fuseaction.

To summarize, the following scenarios are all equivalent ways to implement the fuseaction **main.showGreeting**:

/view/main.cfc:
```
<cfcomponent access="public">
  <cffunction name="showGreeting">
    <cfinclude template="dspHello.cfm" />
  </cffunction>
  <!--- [Functions for other fuseactions here] --->
</cfcomponent>
```
/main/showGreeting.cfc:
```
<cfcomponent access="public">
  <cffunction name="do">
    <cfinclude template="dspHello.cfm" />
  </cffunction>
  <!--- [No other functions ] --->
</cfcomponent>
```
/main/showGreeting.cfm:
```
<cfinclude template="dspHello.cfm">
```

NOTE: Fusebox 5.5 will also use a circuit.xml file if it its found in a circuit-named directory, and use it as though it were in a traditional modern Fusebox application. Since this chapter is about going XML-less, we're not exploring that approach here.

These approaches are shown in detail in the variations of Wegot Widgets shown in later chapters.

Global Fuseactions

Global fuseactions are one of the niceties of traditional modern Fusebox that have to be considered when going without XML. There are several ways to provide global fuseactions, depending on which approach we're taking to circuit configuration.

Regardless of approach, we can get the same effect as a globalPrefuseaction and a globalPostFuseaction by using Application.cfm and OnRequestEnd.cfm, respectively. The same logic is available using the OnRequestStart and OnRequestEnd functions of Application.cfc. When taking this approach (regardless of whether we're using Application.cfc or Application.cfm), It's important to make sure we're setting any values we want for the FUSEBOX_PARAMETERS structure before any global fuseactions. That is, we don't want the FUSEBOX_PARAMETERS initialization in index.cfm, because the Application.cfm code will run before the code in index.cfm, and in the case of Application.cfc, there is no code in index.cfm—it's just a placeholder since Application.cfc extends the Fusebox application component.

Pre- and post-fuseactions at the circuit level are more dependent on the approach taken, as the code that represents these actions must be placed within the circuit framework itself. Therefore, the code's location differs between, for example, an application that uses directories as circuits vs. one that uses CFCs as circuits. Examples of these types of fuseactions also appear in the sample applications in later chapters.

Plugins

Plugins are another issue altogether when it comes to building XML-less Fusebox applications. Put simply, if the application needs to use a plugin, going XML-less isn't an option. Plugins are a feature of the XML-based approach to Fusebox, where the XML-less approach is intended to appeal to fans of earlier versions of Fusebox who don't want to deal in XML-based configuration.

Factor 3: Omitting circuit.xml

The primary purpose in providing an XML-less capability in Fusebox 5 is to avoid the need to explicitly define circuits using XML configuration files. We've already looked at omitting the application configuration file fusebox.xml; the other XML file to be omitted is the circuit configuration file, circuit.xml.

In the traditional modern approach, each circuit has a circuit.xml file. This file contains the configuration of fuseactions contained within that circuit. Fusebox 5.5 allows us to rely on application structure to define fuseactions within circuits. This approach is similar to the way circuits were implied by directory structure in Fusebox prior to version 4.

In Fusebox 5.5, though, circuits can be constructed in several ways. They can be directories that are named according to the circuit names in any of several locations (see the next section). They can also be CFCs named according to the circuit names, also located in any of several location. In either case, we need to be able to define fuseactions within the circuit, just as we did with circuit.xml.

NOTE: Fusebox 5.5 give precedence to circuit.xml, even when using implicitly defined circuits. If circuit.xml exists within a circuit directory, it will be used. Details on this are in the next section.

As an alternative to fuseactions defined in circuit.xml, fuseactions can be defined as ColdFusion templates (cfm) or ColdFusion components (cfc) named according to the fuseaction name. The first method will appeal to traditional CFML developers, while the second method will be preferred by developers wishing to leverage CFCs and more object-based approach.

The Fusebox 5.5 specification also mentions the ability to use fuseactions defined by XML files named for each fuseaction. As of this writing, that ability has been set for future implementation. If a fuseaction is defined using an XML file (named as *fuseaction*.xml), the Fusebox core will throw the error message **An Error of type "fusebox.undefinedFuseaction" has occurred**. This issue has been identified in the Fusebox bug tracking database as Bug #261, deferred to version 5.6 pending feedback from the community. You can voice your opinion on the Bug Tracker page at fusebox.org.

Factor 4: Implicitly Locating a Circuit

The final task accomplished by the XML-based application configuration file is to define where circuits are located and give those locations aliases. When the XML is discarded, this task is basically stood on its head. That is, circuits are defined by where they are located, rather than located according to their definition. In other words, circuits are implicitly defined rather than being explicitly defined by a configuration file.

We've already seen in the preceding paragraphs that circuits can be defined as directories or as CFCs within the application's root directory. When a request is made to the application, Fusebox looks for a directory or CFC that matches the circuit name specified in the request. If such a directory or CFC is found, Fusebox looks for a template or function, respectively, that corresponds to the fuseaction specified in the request. This is how Fusebox 5.5 implicitly locates circuits.

NOTE: In order for Fusebox to implicitly locate circuits without a fusebox.xml file, the setting
FUSEBOX_PARAMETERS.allowImplicitFusebox = true
must appear in the application's Application.cfc.

Precedence

We saw in the previous section that Fusebox 5.5 has the ability to discover circuits implicitly. But where does it look, and for what? The answers to these two questions constitute the order of precedence for circuit discovery. Let's start with the *what* question first, as it's a bit easier to state in a nutshell.

When a Fusebox 5.5 application that has the **allowImplicitFusebox** parameter set to true receives a request, it looks for circuits defined in one of three ways, in the following order:

1. Using a circuit.xml file,

2. Using a CFC named with the circuit's alias, or

3. Using a directory named with the circuit's alias.

So if an application has both a directory named with the alias and a CFC named with the alias, the CFC will take precedence. Now that we know *what* Fusebox is looking for in terms of circuit discovery, let's find out *where* it looks for those things.

Although at first blush it might seem nice to be able to just throw circuits in wherever and however we like and have Fusebox discover them automagically, in reality this practice would run counter to all the basic ideas of Fusebox—organization and simplicity being among them. So Fusebox 5.5 looks in a fixed set of places for each type of circuit defintion. The following sections detail the order of precedence for each type. The prevalence of the Model-View-Controller design pattern in the Fusebox community is apparent.

> **NOTE:** Though these sections refer to the circuit alias, in Fusebox 5.5 the alias is the circuit name. We use the term alias to conform to the terminology established in Fusebox 4, where a circuit could be aliased to a name different from its directory name.

Locating circuit.xml

When searching for a circuit.xml file, Fusebox 5.5 looks for it in the following locations:

controller/[circuitAlias]/
model/[circuitAlias]/
view/[circuitAlias]/
[circuitAlias]/controller/

[circuitAlias]/model/
alias/view/
alias/

Locating a Circuit CFC

When searching for a circuit CFC, Fusebox 5.5 looks for it in the following locations:

controller/[circuitAlias].cfc
model/[circuitAlias].cfc
view/[circuitAlias].cfc

Locating a Circuit Directory

When searching for a circuit directory, Fusebox 5.5 looks for it in the following locations:

controller/[circuitAlias]/
model/[circuitAlias]/
view/[circuitAlias]/
[circuitAlias]/

Only after exhausting all these possibilities does Fusebox throw a "circuit not defined" error.

Putting It Together

Combining explicit or implicit circuit configuration with explicit or implicit fuseaction configuration, we come up with several possible ways to combine the techniques. The following table shows how the various techniques can be used.

Defining Circuits and Fuseactions		Circuit Definition		
		Fusebox.xml	Implicit – Directory	Implicit - Circuit CFC
Fuseaction Definition	circuit.xml	✔	✔	no
	action.xml*	✔	✔	no
	action.cfm	✔	✔	no
	action.cfc	✔	✔	no
	CFC method	no	no	✔

* As of Fusebox 5.5., fuseaction XML files are designated as a future enhancement.

Illustration 10: Combining Circuit and Fuseaction Definition Techniques

Note that within the first two types of circuit configuration (explicit and implicit-directory), any of the various fuseaction configuration techniques can be used. In fact, they can be used in combination within an application, and even within a circuit (though we can't combine explicit and implicit fuseaction configuration techniques within a circuit—the explicit circuit.xml will always override implicit techniques for that circuit).

Summary

When using the "no XML" or XML-less approach to Fusebox 5.5, four factors of the XML configuration files must be replaced. They are Fusebox parameters, replacing the behavior of the application configuration file (fusebox.xml), replacing the behavior of the circuit configuration files (circuit.xml), and implicitly determining the location of circuits.

Chapter 5 – Other New Topics

Fusebox 5.5 brings several new features to Fusebox, including dynamic do, the event object, Application.cfc support, and updates to the myFusebox object. These features bring unprecedented flexibility and information to us as developers. The following sections will present each of these features.

Dynamic Do

In Fusebox 4 and 5, the <do> verb allows execution of any fuseaction as part of another fuseaction. This technique makes Fusebox very flexible in terms of how fuseactions can be constructed.

With the creation of XML-less circuits and fuseactions in Fusebox 5.5, it was desirable to replicate this ability to call a fuseaction as part of another fuseaction. Without the Fusebox XML <do> verb, a new method was required. That method is the do method of the myFusebox object, or the "dynamic do", as it is termed.

With this method, we just change the syntax of a fuseaction call from the <do> verb in XML, like this:

```
<do action="login.showWelcome" />
```
to a statement invoking the do method of the myFusebox object, like this:

```
<cfinvoke object="myFusebox" methodcall="do('login.showWelcome')" />
```
This has a couple of very important implications. First, it means we can execute any fuseaction at any point in our CFML code. It also means that we can construct calls to fuseactions dynamically. Consider this code:

```
<cfscript>
  myFusebox.do(clientType & ".showWelcome")
</cfscript>
```
If the variable clientType was previously set to a value based on the type of client calling the application (such as "browser" or "mobile"), then this statement would automatically request the showWelcome fuseaction from a view circuit appropriate for that client. This is a much more flexible and easy-to-use approach than the conditional logic required in the XML-based approach.

The do() method can take the following arguments:

- fuseaction (string, required)
- contentvariable (string, optional)
- append (boolean, optional, defaults to false)
- returnOutput (boolean, optional, defaults to false)

Providing a contentvariable argument causes the method to store the output of the fuseaction in the specified variable in the top-level variables scope, just as using the contentvariable attribute in the <do> verb. The append argument allows the output to be appended to the specified variable.

The returnOutput argument causes the output of the fuseaction to be returned from the method call, allowing us to store it in a variable of choice. This is the way to go if we want to store the output in something other than a top-level content variable.

The Event Object

With the increased support of CFCs in Fusebox 5, one of the long-time popular techniques of Fusebox came into focus. That technique is the use of the attributes scope to contain all values passed into a fuseaction, regardless of whether they came in via the URL, form submission, or passing as attributes.

When using CFCs, the attributes scope as defined in previous versions of Fusebox isn't available inside CFC methods. So those values must be made available somehow. The event object handles this responsibility while providing some additional nice-to-have features. Fusebox 5.1 introduced the event object, and Fusebox 5.5 expands on its capabilities.

The Fusebox framework automatically creates the event object, allowing it to be passed as an argument into any CFC method. Formally speaking, the event object is an object of type fuseboxEvent. The fuseboxEvent CFC defines the following methods:

- xfa()
  - New to Fusebox 5.5
  - xfa("xfaName","fuseaction") sets xfa value
  - xfa("xfaName") gets xfa value
- setValue()
  - setValue("varName","value") sets variable value
- getAllValues()
  - Returns a structure of all the variable values in the event object
- init()
  - Constructor for the event object. Used by the Fusebox framework.
- getValue()
  - getValue("varName") returns the value of the specified variable.
- valueExists()
  - valueExists("varName") returns yes if the variable exists, otherwise no.
- removeValue()
  - removeValue("varName") removes the variable from the event object

When using CFCs in Fusebox, the first two arguments of a method should be `myFusebox` and `event`. This convention ensures that these objects are available within the scope of the method. Then, instead of referring to `attributes.varName` within the method, we use `event.getValue("varName")` instead.

Application.cfc Support

Fusebox developers are accustomed to invoking the Fusebox framework by its inclusion in Application.cfm or index.cfm. Lately, though, Application.cfc has been gaining in popularity as a more robust alternative to Application.cfm. Fortunately, Fusebox keeps up with the times.

Fusebox 5.5 brings us direct support for Application.cfc by providing the fusebox5.Application CFC. By using Application.cfc to extend fusebox5.Application, we can invoke the Fusebox framework as an integrated part of the processing of Application.cfc. Doing this is as simple as adding the extends attribute to the <cfcomponent> tag in Application.cfc:

```
<cfcomponent extends="fusebox5.Application" output="false">
```

The index.cfm file must still exist, but it can be empty (many developers like to put a comment in it just to explain its presence though it's empty).

There is a critical point that must be followed when using Application.cfc, though. Because the Fusebox application object has methods equating to the methods found in Application.cfc, we **must** invoke the Fusebox (i.e. super) method if we use the method in our Application.cfc. If we don't do this, the Fusebox method won't be executed and things won't work the way we expect them to work.

Here's an example of how the onRequestStart method would look in Application.cfc for a Fusebox application:

```
<cffunction name="onRequestStart">
   <cfargument name="myPage" />
   <cfset super.onRequestStart(arguments.myPage) />
   <!--- Additional code --->
</cffunction>
```

Adding in this simple bit of code on top of the method takes care of it. The onRequestStart method in the Fusebox application CFC is run, then the code in the specific in the Application.cfc method (following the super call) is run.

myFusebox Updates

The myFusebox object gets some new capabilities in Fusebox 5.5. These updates make it easier than ever to keep track of what's going on in an application at any given time.

showDebug Property

The showDebug property is a boolean value that defaults to true. It can be updated programmatically to suppress debug output for any given fuseaction. We just set the value of the property to false to suppress debug output:

```
<cfset myFusebox.showDebug = false>
```

More productively, we can set the value of the property based on some condition:

```
<cfset myFusebox.showDebug = myFusebox.variables()._FBA.mode EQ "development">
```

NOTE: The showDebug property is only active if the Fusebox debug parameter is set to true.

getApplicationData() Method

This method is a simplification over the syntax required in Fusebox 5.1 to retrieve the application's complete data structure. The method has been moved from the application object over to the myFusebox object. Where in the previous version we had to use

```
<cfset myData = myFusebox.getApplication().getApplicationData()>
```

in Fusebox 5.5, this is simplified to just

```
<cfset myData = myFusebox.getApplicationData()>
```

The previous method still works, but the new method is an easier-to-follow shortcut to the same result.

getOriginalCircuit() Method

This method returns the original circuit object for the request. It is similar in use to the `getCurrentCircuit()` method, but returns the original circuit instead of the current circuit. Thus, if we execute this method is part of a `<do>` within a fuseaction, this method will return the circuit of the fuseaction that called the `<do>`, whereas `getCurrentCircuit()` will return the circuit of the fuseaction specified in the `<do>`. Keep in mind that this method returns the circuit object, not the circuit's name.

getOriginalFuseaction() Method

This method returns the original fuseaction object for the request. It is similar in use to the `getCurrentFuseaction()` method, but returns the original fuseaction instead of the current fuseaction. Thus, if we execute this method is part of a `<do>` within a fuseaction, this method will return the fuseaction that called the `<do>`, whereas `getCurrentFuseaction()` will return the fuseaction specified in the `<do>`. Keep in mind that this method returns the fuseaction object, not the fuseaction's name.

variables() Method

This method returns the entire top-level variables structure. As such, it can be a valuable means of inspecting the whole goings-on within an application. Take care, though—this can be a rather large structure, even for simple applications. For example, the following illustration shows the result of dumping myFusebox.variables() for the WegotWidgets Basic application. It is NOT recommended that you try to actually read the text!

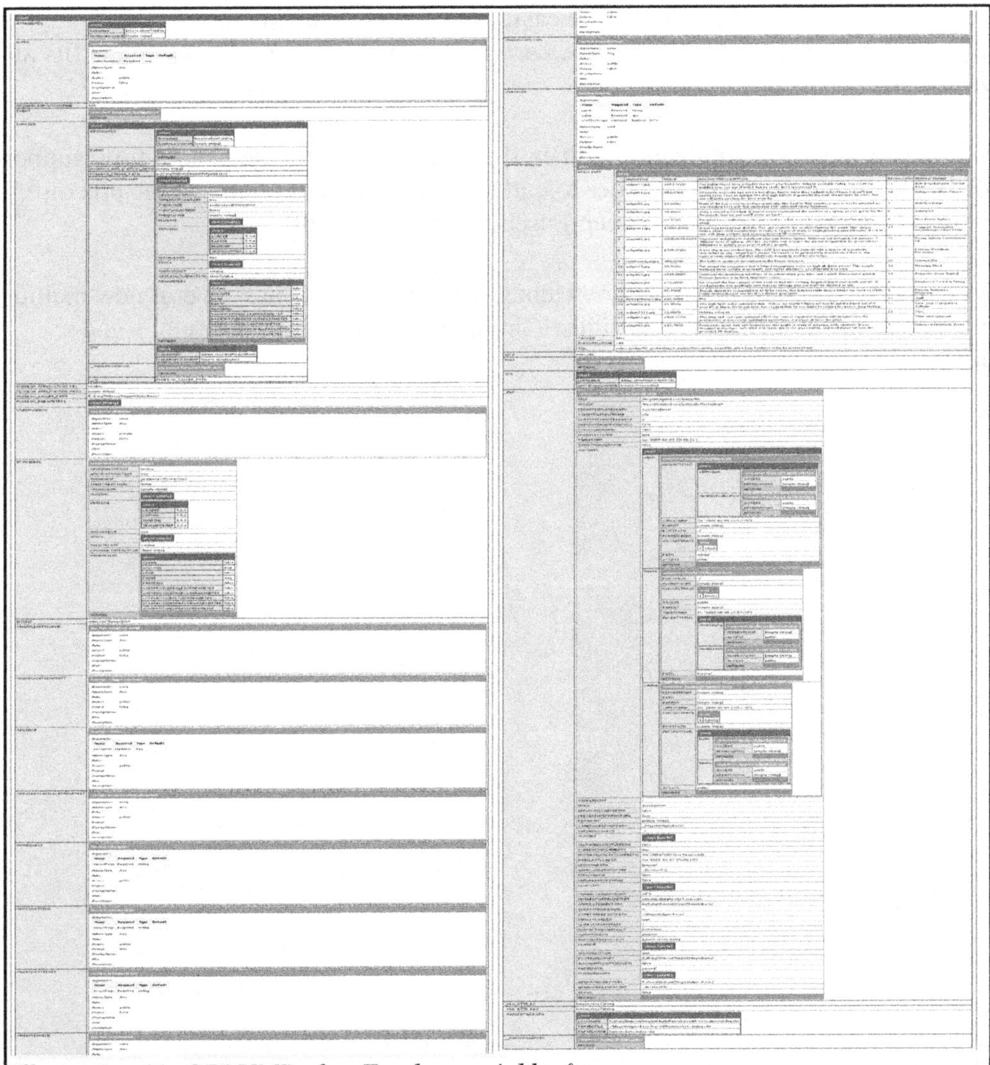

Illustration 11: CFDUMP of myFusebox.variables()

Summary

The ability to execute dynamic do commands is one of the new features of Fusebox 5.5. We are no longer constrained to calling other fuseactions from within the circuit.xml file.

The event object allows information to be easily passed into CFC methods. It also replicates the traditional attributes scope in Fusebox, carrying on the tradition of "one scope fits all" for input variables..

By extending the Fusebox application object, the Application.cfc file is now fully supported in Fusebox. It is important to remember to call the super method of any of the preconfigured Application.cfc methods in order to keep Fusebox behaving well.

The myFusebox object has the new showDebug property. It also has several new methods, including getApplicationData(), getOriginalCircuit(), getOriginalFuseaction(), and variables().

Chapter 6 – Directories as Circuits: Circuit.xml

The Wegot Widgets application is a reference application: one that is designed to be very simple while demonstrating most of the basic concepts of an application: displaying database content, refining that content (e.g. selecting a single product from a list of products), accepting user input, and storing input to the database.

The application consists of two circuits. The **browse** circuit presents a catalog list of products, from which the user can select a product to see details about that product. There is also a link to an Admin page. The second circuit, **admin**, presents a form to allow addition of a new item to the database, and also processes that form's data into the database, including upload of a photo file. The following illustration maps this simple application's fuseactions.

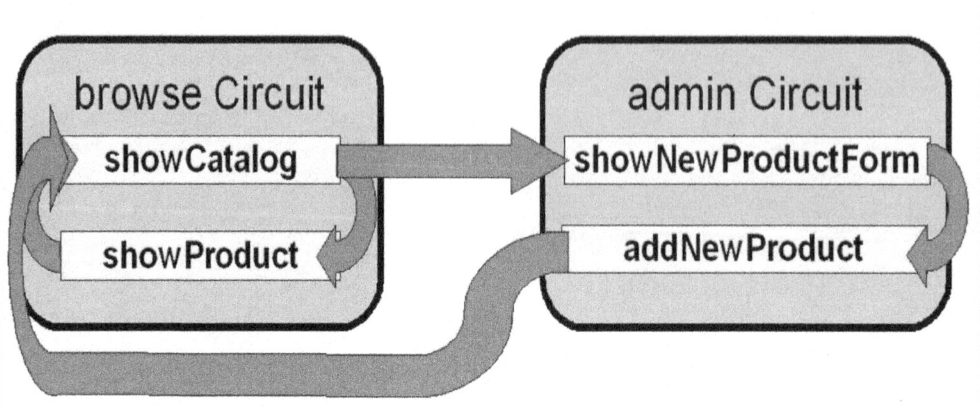

Illustration 12: Wegot Widgets Fuseaction Map

This first sample application version of Wegot Widgets is only a partial excursion into Fusebox 5 without XML. It does away with the application configuration file (fusebox.xml) in favor of implicit circuits defined by directories. Within each circuit, though, the configuration sticks with using a circuit.xml file to define the fuseactions.

We'll step through the important parts of the application, taking a look at how this approach differs from the other "no-XML" approaches presented in the book. First, let's look at how this application is laid out.

Application Map

The application map for this approach is shown in the following illustration. The parsed directory is closed because we don't need to see what Fusebox builds—just the parts we're responsible for writing.

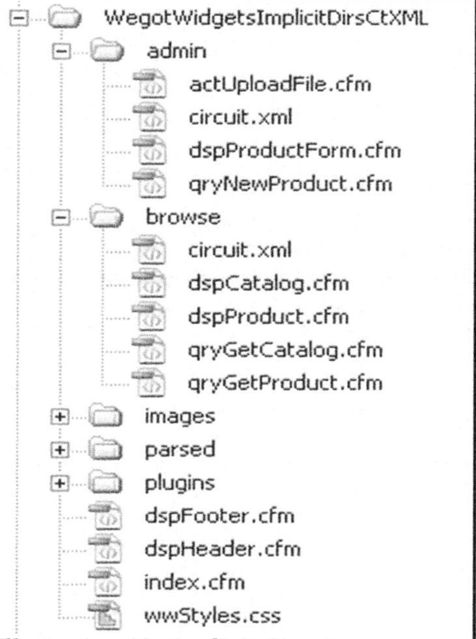

Illustration 13: Implicit Circuit Directories with Circuit.xml Files

There are just two circuits in the application: admin and browse. The following sections discuss how the application's critical parts work, starting with the application configuration.

Application Configuration

Since there's no fusebox.xml file, the application configuration relies on conventions rather than a configuration file. As with any ColdFusion application, we start with index.cfm, and Application.cfm or Application.cfc. In the case of this sample app, the work is handled in index.cfm.

```
<!--- index.cfm for WegotWidgetsImplicitDirsCtXML --->
<cfapplication
  name="WegotWidgetsImplicitDirsCtXML"
  sessionmanagement="Yes"
  sessiontimeout="#CreateTimeSpan(0,0,30,0)#"
  clientmanagement="Yes">
<cfscript>
  FUSEBOX_APPLICATION_PATH = ""
  // must enable implicit (no-XML) mode!
  FUSEBOX_PARAMETERS.allowImplicitFusebox = true;
  FUSEBOX_PARAMETERS.defaultFuseaction = "browse.showCatalog";
  FUSEBOX_PARAMETERS.mode = "development-full-load";
  FUSEBOX_PARAMETERS.conditionalParse = true;
  // change this to something more secure:
  FUSEBOX_PARAMETERS.password = "";
  FUSEBOX_PARAMETERS.strictMode = true;
  FUSEBOX_PARAMETERS.debug = true;
  FUSEBOX_PARAMETERS.errortemplatesPath = "/fusebox551/errortemplates/";
  dsn = "WegotWidgets";
  self = "index.cfm";
  myself = "#self#?fuseaction=";
</cfscript>

<cfinclude template="dspHeader.cfm">
<cfinclude template="/fusebox551/fusebox5.cfm">
<cfinclude template="dspFooter.cfm">
```

The first part of index.cfm is just a typical <cfapplication> tag. Then we start getting into the Fusebox-related parts. The <cfscript> block sets up the Fusebox parameters that would have been defined in fusebox.xml. Because we're not defining circuits explicitly, the allowImplicitFusebox parameter must be set to **true**.

Finally, the application takes an old-school approach to presenting a header and footer: they are just included before and after the call to the Fusebox core.

Default Fuseaction

As it would be if we were using fusebox.xml, the default fuseaction is set with the defaultFuseaction parameter. The difference in the no-XML is that this parameter is set in CFML instead of in XML. The choice to place the CFML in index.cfm is arbitrary. We could just as well have chosen to use Application.cfm or Application.cfc for the same purpose.

Parameters

As shown in the code section, the Fusebox parameters are also set in CFML instead of in XML. The only caveat is to make sure parameters are set before the Fusebox core is called. In the case of using Application.cfc, which extends the Fusebox application CFC, the parameters are set in the CFC's initialization section, before any <cffunction> declarations.

Circuit Definition

Circuit definition is the most obvious difference between the traditional modern approach to Fusebox and the no-XML approach. Without a fusebox.xml file, there is no <circuits> section to set up the circuit/alias configuration.

Fusebox 5.5 could have taken an approach similar to versions of Fusebox prior to 4, using CFML to set up the circuit definitions. But Sean made a decision to have the Fusebox 5.5 framework be a little more helpful to developers. So instead of just substituting a CFML-based version of circuit definition for the XML, Fusebox 5.5 figures out what the circuits are all by itself.

The details of how Fusebox does this are found in Chapter 4. For this particular sample application, the circuits are simply directories under the root of the application. So when a fuseaction with a circuit of **browse** is requested, Fusebox sees that a directory named "browse" exists under the application root, and uses that directory as the circuit. If a fuseaction is called for which no circuit can be deduced, Fusebox will throw a "circuit not defined" error.

Initialization

The Fusebox framework is initialized in the approach by including the core's base file, fusebox5.cfm. But an important part of the initialization process is setting the Fusebox parameters, which takes place before the core is included. It sounds a bit like beating a dead horse, but the relationship between parameters and the core is critical. If we call the core before the parameters have been established, we'll get unexpected behavior based on the default settings for each parameter.

This particular sample application calls the core's base file from index.cfm.

Fuseaction Definition

In this particular sample, fuseactions are defined just as in a traditional modern Fusebox application: with a circuit.xml file for each circuit. This sample's circuit.xml files are shown below, **admin** circuit followed by the **browse** circuit.

```
<circuit access="public">
  <fuseaction name="addProduct">
    <include template="actUploadFile" />
    <include template="qryNewProduct" />
    <do action="browse.showCatalog" />
  </fuseaction>
  <fuseaction name="showNewProductForm">
    <xfa name="submitForm" value="admin.addProduct" />
    <include template="dspProductForm" />
  </fuseaction>
</circuit>
<circuit access="public">
  <fuseaction name="showCatalog">
    <xfa name="lnkProductName" value="browse.showProduct" />
    <xfa name="lnkAdmin" value="admin.showNewProductForm" />
    <include template="qryGetCatalog" />
    <include template="dspCatalog"/>
  </fuseaction>
  <fuseaction name="showProduct">
    <xfa name="lnkBackToCatalog" value="browse.showCatalog" />
    <include template="qryGetProduct" />
    <include template="dspProduct" />
  </fuseaction>
</circuit>
```

Although it may seem contrary to the "no-XML" philosophy to allow circuit.xml files to be used with an application that has no fusebox.xml file, it makes sense to differentiate between application configuration and circuit configuration. Based on that point of view, we should be able to exercise any of the options for circuit configuration, regardless of the chosen approach to application configuration. It's likely that anyone choosing no to use XML for their application configuration will probably make the same choice regarding circuit configuration, but the choice remains open.

Summary

This sample application demonstrates the use of implicit circuits defined by directory names, with fuseactions defined by the use of a circuit.xml file in each circuit directory. Fusebox parameters are set in index.cfm, though Application.cfm or Application.cfc could also be used (see other sample chapters). The Fusebox framework is initialized by including the initial core file, fusebox5.cfm, from index.cfm. Each fuseaction is defined with its own

<fuseaction> section in its circuit's circuit.xml file. Using circuit.xml files in an application without a fusebox.xml file may seem illogical, but is included here to show all possibilities.

The next chapter shows the sample application with implicit circuits defined by directories and imp.licit fuseactions defined by CFML templates.

Chapter 7 – Directories as Circuits: CFM Fuseactions

The Wegot Widgets application is a reference application: one that is designed to be very simple while demonstrating most of the basic concepts of an application: displaying database content, refining that content (e.g. selecting a single product from a list of products), accepting user input, and storing input to the database.

The application consists of two circuits. The **browse** circuit presents a catalog list of products, from which the user can select a product to see details about that product. There is also a link to an Admin page. The second circuit, **admin**, presents a form to allow addition of a new item to the database, and also processes that form's data into the database, including upload of a photo file. The following illustration maps this simple application's fuseactions.

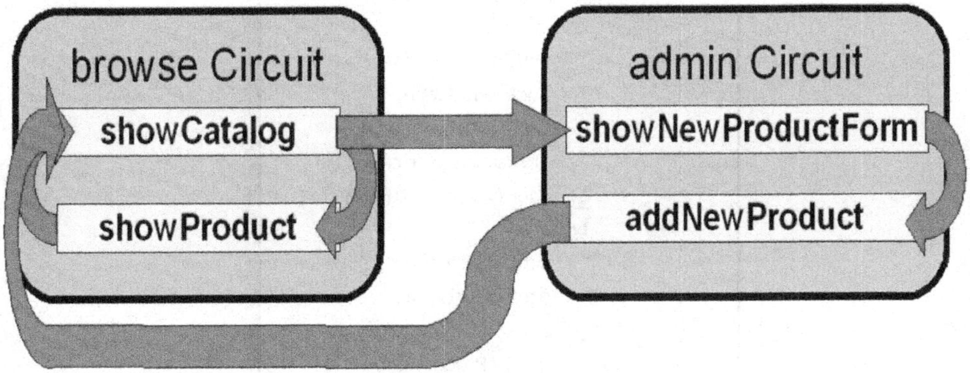

Illustration 14: Wegot Widgets Fuseaction Map

This second sample application version of Wegot Widgets demonstrates a completely XML-free approach to Fusebox 5. It does away with the application configuration file (fusebox.xml) in favor of implicit circuits defined by directories. Within each circuit, fuseactions are defined by CFML templates named for the particular fuseaction. For example, the fuseaction browse.showCatalog is defined by a template named **showCatalog.cfm** in a directory named **browse**.

We'll step through the important parts of the application, taking a look at how this approach differs from the other "no-XML" approaches presented in the book. First, let's look at how this application is laid out.

Application Map

The application map for this approach is shown in the following illustration. The parsed directory is closed because we don't need to see what Fusebox builds—just the parts we're responsible for writing.

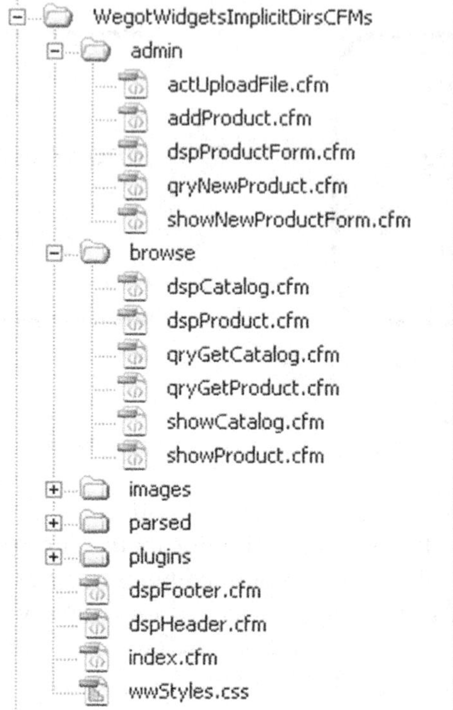

Illustration 15: Implicit Circuit Directories with Fuseaction CFM Files

There are just two circuits in the application: admin and browse. The following sections discuss how the application's critical parts work, starting with the application configuration.

Application Configuration

Since there's no fusebox.xml file, the application configuration relies on conventions rather than a configuration file. As with any ColdFusion application, we start with index.cfm, and Application.cfm or Application.cfc. In the case of this sample app, the work is handled in index.cfm.

```
<!--- index.cfm for WegotWidgetsImplicitDirsCFM --->
<cfapplication
   name="WegotWidgetsImplicitDirsCFM"
   sessionmanagement="Yes"
   sessiontimeout="#CreateTimeSpan(0,0,30,0)#"
   clientmanagement="Yes">
<cfscript>
   FUSEBOX_APPLICATION_PATH = ""
   // must enable implicit (no-XML) mode!
   FUSEBOX_PARAMETERS.allowImplicitFusebox = true;
   FUSEBOX_PARAMETERS.defaultFuseaction = "browse.showCatalog";
   FUSEBOX_PARAMETERS.mode = "development-full-load";
   FUSEBOX_PARAMETERS.conditionalParse = true;
   // change this to something more secure:
   FUSEBOX_PARAMETERS.password = "";
   FUSEBOX_PARAMETERS.strictMode = true;
   FUSEBOX_PARAMETERS.debug = true;
   FUSEBOX_PARAMETERS.errortemplatesPath = "/fusebox551/errortemplates/";
   FUSEBOX_PARAMETERS.allowImplicitCircuits = true;
   dsn = "WegotWidgets";
   self = "index.cfm";
   myself = "#self#?fuseaction=";
</cfscript>

<cfinclude template="dspHeader.cfm">
<cfinclude template="/fusebox551/fusebox5.cfm">
<cfinclude template="dspFooter.cfm">
```

The first part of index.cfm is just a typical <cfapplication> tag. Then we start getting into the Fusebox-related parts. The <cfscript> block sets up the Fusebox parameters that would have been defined in fusebox.xml. Because we're not defining circuits with an explicit fusebox.xml file, the allowImplicitFusebox parameter must be set to **true**. Because we're not defining fuseactions with explicit circuit.xml files, the allowImplicitCircuits parameter must also be set to **true**.

Finally, the application takes an old-school approach to presenting a header and footer: they are just included before and after the call to the Fusebox core.

Default Fuseaction

As it would be if we were using fusebox.xml, the default fuseaction is set with the defaultFuseaction parameter. The difference in the no-XML is that this parameter is set in CFML instead of in XML. The choice to place the CFML in index.cfm is arbitrary. We could just as well have chosen to use Application.cfm or Application.cfc for the same purpose.

Parameters

As shown in the code section, the Fusebox parameters are also set in CFML instead of in XML. The only caveat is to make sure parameters are set before the Fusebox core is called. In the case of using Application.cfc, which extends the Fusebox application CFC, the parameters are set in the CFC's initialization section, before any <cffunction> declarations.

Circuit Definition

Circuit definition is the most obvious difference between the traditional modern approach to Fusebox and the no-XML approach. Without a fusebox.xml file, there is no <circuits> section to set up the circuit/alias configuration.

Fusebox 5.5 could have taken an approach similar to versions of Fusebox prior to 4, using CFML to set up the circuit definitions. But Sean made a decision to have the Fusebox 5.5 framework be a little more helpful to developers. So instead of just substituting a CFML-based version of circuit definition for the XML, Fusebox 5.5 figures out what the circuits are all by itself.

The details of how Fusebox does this are found in Chapter 4. For this particular sample application, the circuits are simply directories under the root of the application. So when a fuseaction with a circuit of **browse** is requested, Fusebox sees that a directory named "browse" exists under the application root, and uses that directory as the circuit. If a fuseaction is called for which no circuit can be deduced, Fusebox will throw a "circuit not defined" error.

Initialization

The Fusebox framework is initialized in the approach by including the core's base file, fusebox5.cfm. But an important part of the initialization process is setting the Fusebox parameters, which takes place before the core is included. It sounds a bit like beating a dead horse, but the relationship between parameters and the core is critical. If we call the core before the parameters have been established, we'll get unexpected behavior based on the default settings for each parameter.

This particular sample application calls the core's base file from index.cfm.

Fuseaction Definition

In this particular sample, fuseactions are defined by CFML templates, one for each fuseaction. This sample's fuseaction files are shown below, **admin** circuit followed by the **browse** circuit.

```
<!--- admin circuit --->

<!--- addProduct.cfm --->
<cfinclude template="actUploadFile.cfm" />
<cfinclude template="qryNewProduct.cfm" />
<cflocation url="index.cfm?fuseaction=browse.showCatalog" />

<!--- showNewProductForm.cfm --->
<cfset xfa.submitForm = "admin.addProduct" />
<cfinclude template="dspProductForm.cfm" />

<!--- browse circuit --->

<!--- showCatalog.cfm --->
<cfset xfa.lnkProductName = "browse.showProduct" />
<cfset xfa.lnkAdmin = "Admin.showNewProductForm" />
<cfinclude template="qryGetCatalog.cfm" />
<cfinclude template="dspCatalog.cfm"/>

<!--- showProduct.cfm --->
<cfset xfa.lnkBackToCatalog = "browse.showCatalog" />
<cfinclude template="qryGetProduct.cfm" />
<cfinclude template="dspProduct.cfm" />
```

This approach to fuseaction configuration appeals to developers who would rather not deal with XML as an added layer in their applications. There is an important feature of Fusebox lost when taking this approach, though: the "roadmap" nature of the circuit definition file. That is, when looking at a circuit configuration file, we can easily sum up the entire operation of the circuit, since all the fuseactions' behavior are clearly presented. When using individual templates for each fuseaction, we have to go through the content of each fuseaction file in order to deduce the flow of the circuit. Also, it can be difficult to differentiate between fuseaction templates and fuse templates—though this could be alleviated by the use of a prefix for fuseaction files, just as we do for query, display, and action fuses.

Summary

This sample application demonstrates the use of implicit circuits defined by directory names, with fuseactions implied by the use of CFML templates. Fusebox parameters are set in index.cfm, though Application.cfm or Application.cfc could also be used (see other sample chapters). The Fusebox framework is initialized by including the initial core file, fusebox5.cfm, from index.cfm. Each fuseaction is defined with its own CFML template named for that fuseaction.

The next chapter shows the sample application with implicit circuits defined by directories and imp.licit fuseactions defined by ColdFusion components (CFCs).

Chapter 8 – Directories as Circuits: CFC Fuseactions

The Wegot Widgets application is a reference application: one that is designed to be very simple while demonstrating most of the basic concepts of an application: displaying database content, refining that content (e.g. selecting a single product from a list of products), accepting user input, and storing input to the database.

The application consists of two logical circuits. The **browse** circuit presents a catalog list of products, from which the user can select a product to see details about that product. There is also a link to an Admin page. The second circuit, **admin**, presents a form to allow addition of a new item to the database, and also processes that form's data into the database, including upload of a photo file.

This particular implementation of Wegot Widgets also presents an explicit Model-View-Controller (MVC) approach. In this approach, each logical circuit is divided into a controller circuit, a model circuit, and a view circuit. The controller circuit is the only one with fuseactions presented to the public. The model and view circuits' fuseactions are internal--called only by the controller circuit. The model circuit is responsible for interaction with the database—the data model. The view circuit is responsible for presenting what the user sees —the view of the application.

The following illustration maps this simple application's fuseactions.

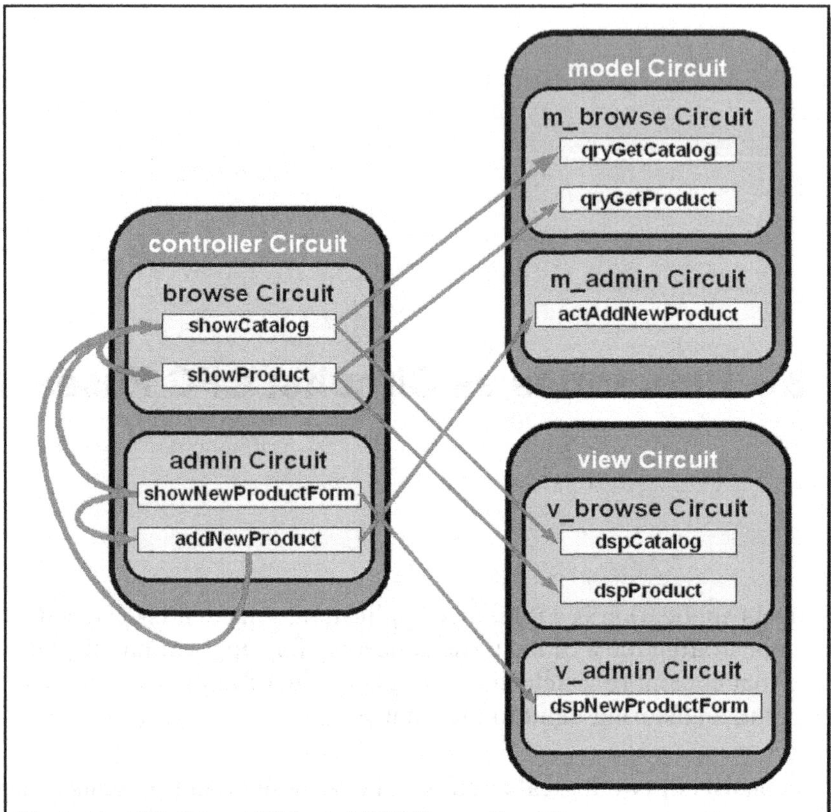

Illustration 16: Wegot Widgets MVC Fuseaction Map

This third sample application version of Wegot Widgets demonstrates a completely XML-free approach to Fusebox 5. It does away with the application configuration file (fusebox.xml) in favor of implicit circuits defined by directories. Within each circuit, fuseactions are defined by CFCs named for the particular fuseaction. For example, the fuseaction browse.showCatalog is defined by a template named **showCatalog.cfc** in a directory named **browse**. Additionally, due to the MVC nature of the implementation, the **browse** directory is found within the **controller** directory.

We'll step through the important parts of the application, taking a look at how this approach differs from the other "no-XML" approaches presented in the book. First, let's look at how this application is laid out.

Application Map

The application map for this approach is shown in the following illustration. The parsed directory is closed because we don't need to see what Fusebox builds—just the parts we're responsible for writing. The fuse files in the m_ and v_ circuits have also been removed to save space in this illustration.

Illustration 17: Implicit Circuit Directories with Fuseaction CFM Files

Even though the logical circuits remain the same as the other samples in this book, the number of circuit directories has tripled, since there's a mode, view, and controller for each logical circuit. The following sections discuss how the application's critical parts work, starting with the application configuration.

Application Configuration

Since there's no fusebox.xml file, the application configuration relies on conventions rather than a configuration file. As with any ColdFusion application, we start with index.cfm, and Application.cfm or Application.cfc. In the case of this sample app, the work is handled in index.cfm and Application.cfc.

> **NOTE:** This logic could all be placed in Application.cfc. The use of index.cfm is purely one of choice.

```
<!--- index.cfm for WegotWidgetsImplicitDirsCFC --->
<cfapplication
   name="WegotWidgetsImplicitDirsCFC"
   sessionmanagement="Yes"
   sessiontimeout="#CreateTimeSpan(0,0,30,0)#"
   clientmanagement="Yes">
<cfset FUSEBOX_APPLICATION_PATH = "">
```

```
<!--- Application.cfc for WegotWidgetsImplicitDirsCFC --->
<cfcomponent extends="fusebox5.Application" output="false">
   <!--- trap non-index.cfm requests - must be outside onXxxYyy() handlers --->
   <cfif right(cgi.script_name, len("index.cfm")) neq "index.cfm" and right(cgi.script_name, 3) neq "cfc">
      <cflocation url="index.cfm" addtoken="no" />
   </cfif>
   <!--- set application name based on the directory path --->
   <cfset this.name = right(REReplace(expandPath('.'),'[^A-Za-z]','','all'),64) />
   <cfset this.sessionManagement = true />

   <cfscript>
      // must enable implicit (no-XML) mode!
      FUSEBOX_PARAMETERS.allowImplicitFusebox = true;
      FUSEBOX_PARAMETERS.defaultFuseaction = "browse.showCatalog";
      FUSEBOX_PARAMETERS.mode = "development-full-load";
      FUSEBOX_PARAMETERS.conditionalParse = true;
      // change this to something more secure:
      FUSEBOX_PARAMETERS.password = "";
      FUSEBOX_PARAMETERS.strictMode = true;
      FUSEBOX_PARAMETERS.debug = true;
      // we use the core file error templates:
      FUSEBOX_PARAMETERS.errortemplatesPath = "/fusebox551/errortemplates/";
   </cfscript>

   <cffunction name="onFuseboxApplicationStart">
      <cfset super.onFuseboxApplicationStart() />
      <cfset dsn="WegotWidgets" />
      <cfset self="index.cfm" />
      <cfset myself="#self#?fuseaction=" />
   </cffunction>

   <cffunction name="onRequestStart">
      <cfargument name="targetPage" />
      <cfset super.onRequestStart(arguments.targetPage) />
      <cfinclude template="dspHeader.cfm">
   </cffunction>

  <cffunction name="onRequestEnd">
      <cfargument name="targetPage" />
      <cfset super.onRequestEnd(arguments.targetPage) />
      <cfinclude template="dspHeader.cfm">
  </cffunction>
</cfcomponent>
```

Index.cfm just uses a typical <cfapplication> tag, then sets the FUSEBOX_APPLICATION_PATH variable. The majority of the application configuration takes place in the Application.cfc file.

In Application.cfc, there are a couple of important things to note. First is that the <cfcomponent> tag extends the Fusebox application component. We'll look at this again in a later section. Second, the Fusebox-related configuration code falls in the component's initialization section—before any <cffunction> blocks. The <cfscript> block sets up the Fusebox parameters that would have been defined in fusebox.xml. Because we're not defining circuits with an explicit fusebox.xml file, the allowImplicitFusebox parameter must be set to **true**.

Finally, the application uses the OnRequestStart and OnRequestEnd methods to present a header and footer. Rather than using fuseactions, they are just included as CFML templates in their respective methods. As such, the header and footer can be viewed as being outside the Fusebox application. Instead, they are treated somewhat as wrappers for the entire application. In a more complex application, we would use content variables and a layout fuseaction to present the final layout.

Default Fuseaction

As it would be if we were using fusebox.xml, the default fuseaction is set with the defaultFuseaction parameter. The difference in the no-XML is that this parameter is set in CFML instead of in XML. The choice to place the CFML in Appliction.cfc is arbitrary. We could just as well have chosen to use index.cfm or Application.cfm for the same purpose.

Parameters

As shown in the code section, the Fusebox parameters are also set in CFML instead of in XML. The only caveat is to make sure parameters are set before the Fusebox core is called. Since we're using Application.cfc, which extends the Fusebox application CFC, the parameters are set in the CFC's initialization section, before any <cffunction> declarations.

Circuit Definition

Circuit definition is the most obvious difference between the traditional modern approach to Fusebox and the no-XML approach. Without a fusebox.xml file, there is no <circuits> section to set up the circuit/alias configuration.

Fusebox 5.5 could have taken an approach similar to versions of Fusebox prior to 4, using CFML to set up the circuit definitions. But Sean made a decision to have the Fusebox 5.5 framework be a little more helpful to developers. So instead of just substituting a CFML-based version of circuit definition for the XML, Fusebox 5.5 figures out what the circuits are all by itself.

The details of how Fusebox does this are found in Chapter 4. For this particular sample application, the circuits are directories under the special directories “controller”, “model”, and “view”. So when a fuseaction with a circuit of **browse** is requested, Fusebox sees that a directory named “browse” exists under the controller directory, and uses that directory as the circuit. If a fuseaction is called for which no circuit can be deduced, Fusebox will throw a “circuit not defined” error.

Initialization

The Fusebox framework is initialized in this approach by the fact that Application.cfc extends the Fusebox application CFC. The code that falls within Application.cfc before any `<cffunction>` blocks constitutes the application's initialization code.

Fuseaction Definition

In this particular sample, fuseactions are defined by CFCs, one for each fuseaction. When using this approach, each CFC has one function named **do**. This sample's fuseaction files are shown below, organized by circuit.

```
<!--- controller/admin/addProduct.cfc --->
<cfcomponent access="public">
  <cffunction name="do">
    <cfargument name="myFusebox" />
    <cfargument name="event" />
    <cfset myFusebox.do("m_admin.actAddNewProduct") />
    <cfset myFusebox.do("browse.showCatalog") />
  </cffunction>
</cfcomponent>

<!--- controller/admin/showNewProductForm.cfc --->
<cfcomponent access="public">
  <cffunction name="do">
    <cfargument name="myFusebox" />
    <cfargument name="event" />
    <cfset event.xfa("submitForm","admin.addNewProduct") />
    <cfset myFusebox.do("v_admin.dspNewProductForm") />
  </cffunction>
</cfcomponent>

<!--- controller/browse/showCatalog.cfc --->
<cfcomponent access="public">
  <cffunction name="do">
    <cfargument name="myFusebox" />
    <cfargument name="event" />
    <cfset event.xfa("lnkProductName","browse.showProduct") />
    <cfset event.xfa("lnkAdmin","admin.showNewProductForm") />
    <cfset event.qryGetCatalog = myFusebox.do("m_browse.qryGetCatalog") />
    <cfset myFusebox.do("v_browse.dspCatalog") />
  </cffunction>
</cfcomponent>

<!--- controller/browse/showProduct.cfc --->
<cfcomponent access="public">
  <cffunction name="do">
    <cfargument name="myFusebox" />
    <cfargument name="event" />
    <cfset event.xfa('lnkBackToCatalog','browse.showCatalog')>
    <cfset event.qryGetProduct = myFusebox.do("m_browse.qryGetProduct") />
    <cfset myFusebox.do("v_browse.dspProduct") />
  </cffunction>
</cfcomponent>

<!--- model/m_admin/actNewProduct.cfc --->
<cfcomponent access="internal">
  <cffunction name="do">
    <cfargument name="myFusebox" />
    <cfargument name="event" />
    <cfinclude template="actUploadPicture.cfm">
    <cfinclude template="actAddNewProduct.cfm">
```

```
  </cffunction>
</cfcomponent>

<!--- model/m_browse/qryGetCatalog.cfc --->
<cfcomponent access="internal">
  <cffunction name="do">
    <cfargument name="myFusebox" />
    <cfargument name="event" />
    <cfinclude template="qryGetCatalog.cfm">
    <cfset event.setValue("qryGetCatalog", qryGetCatalog)>
  </cffunction>
</cfcomponent>

<!--- model/m_browse/qryGetProduct.cfc --->
<cfcomponent access="internal">
  <cffunction name="do">
    <cfargument name="myFusebox" />
    <cfargument name="event" />
    <cfinclude template="qryGetProduct.cfm">
    <cfset event.setValue("qryGetProduct", qryGetProduct)>
  </cffunction>
</cfcomponent>

<!--- view/v_admin/dspNewProductForm.cfc --->
<cfcomponent access="internal">
  <cffunction name="do">
    <cfargument name="myFusebox" />
    <cfargument name="event" />
    <cfset attributes = myFusebox.variables()>
    <cfinclude template="dspNewProductForm.cfm">
  </cffunction>
</cfcomponent>

<!--- view/v_browse/dspCatalog.cfc --->
<cfcomponent access="internal">
  <cffunction name="do">
    <cfargument name="myFusebox" />
    <cfargument name="event" />
    <cfset attributes = myFusebox.variables()>
    <cfset qryGetCatalog = attributes.attributes.qryGetCatalog>
    <cfinclude template="dspCatalog.cfm">
  </cffunction>
</cfcomponent>

<!--- view/v_browse/dspProduct.cfc --->
<cfcomponent access="internal">
  <cffunction name="do">
    <cfargument name="myFusebox" />
    <cfargument name="event" />
    <cfset attributes = myFusebox.variables()>
```

```
    <cfset qryGetProduct = attributes.attributes.qryGetProduct>
    <cfinclude template="dspProduct.cfm">
  </cffunction>
</cfcomponent>
```

This approach to fuseaction configuration appeals to developers who are comfortable with CFCs. Although the model in this application doesn't feature CFCs that represent data constructs as a more object-oriented application would, it takes advantage of the difference between public and internal components to provide added security and robustness. It also allows the architect to work in CFCs while the fuse programmers still work in plain old CFML fuse files.

Summary

This sample application demonstrates the use of implicit circuits defined by directory names, with fuseactions implied by the use of ColdFusion components. Fusebox parameters are set in Application.cfc, though Application.cfm or index.cfm could also be used (see other sample chapters). The Fusebox framework is initialized by using Application.cfc to extend the Fusebox application component. Each fuseaction is defined with its own CFC named for that fuseaction.

The next chapter shows the sample application with implicit circuits defined by ColdFusion components (CFCs), with fuseactions defined as methods within those components

.

Chapter 9 – CFCs as Circuits

The Wegot Widgets application is a reference application: one that is designed to be very simple while demonstrating most of the basic concepts of an application: displaying database content, refining that content (e.g. selecting a single product from a list of products), accepting user input, and storing input to the database.

The application consists of two logical circuits. The **browse** circuit presents a catalog list of products, from which the user can select a product to see details about that product. There is also a link to an Admin page. The second circuit, **admin**, presents a form to allow addition of a new item to the database, and also processes that form's data into the database, including upload of a photo file.

This particular implementation of Wegot Widgets also presents an explicit Model-View-Controller (MVC) approach. In this approach, each logical circuit is divided into a controller circuit, a model circuit, and a view circuit. The controller circuit is the only one with fuseactions presented to the public. The model and view circuits' fuseactions are internal--called only by the controller circuit. The model circuit is responsible for interaction with the database—the data model. The view circuit is responsible for presenting what the user sees—the view of the application.

The following illustration maps this simple application's fuseactions.

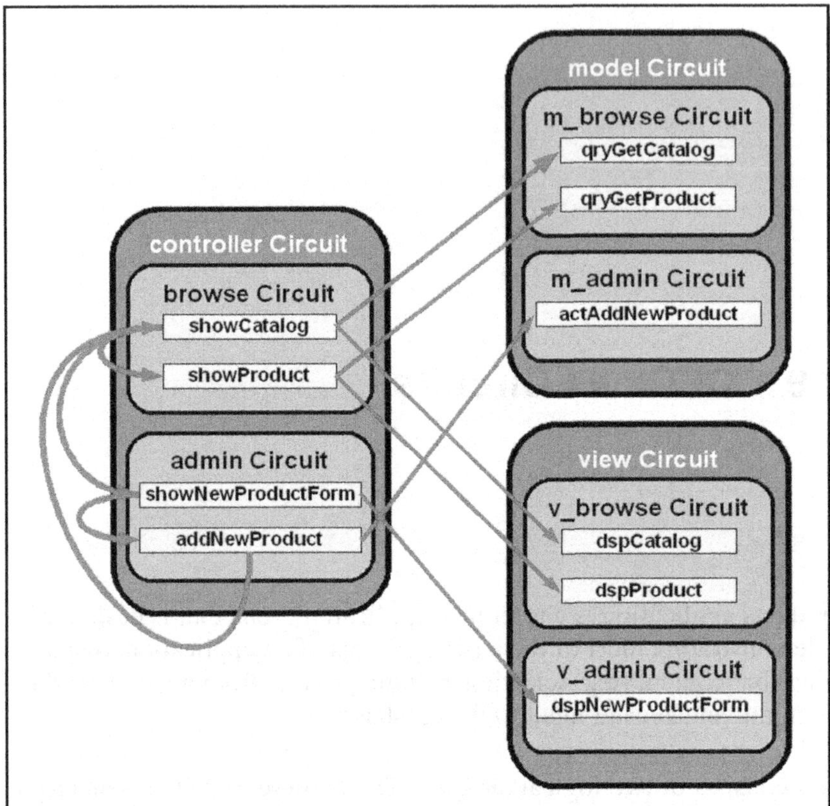

Illustration 18: Wegot Widgets MVC Fuseaction Map

This third sample application version of Wegot Widgets demonstrates a completely XML-free approach to Fusebox 5. It does away with the application configuration file (fusebox.xml) in favor of implicit circuits defined by a CFC named for each circuit. Within each circuit, fuseactions are defined by methods (cffunctions) named for the particular fuseaction. For example, the fuseaction browse.showCatalog is defined by a CFC named **browse.cfc**. Additionally, due to the MVC nature of the implementation, the **browse** circuit CFC is found within the **controller** directory.

We'll step through the important parts of the application, taking a look at how this approach differs from the other "no-XML" approaches presented in the book. First, let's look at how this application is laid out.

Application Map

The application map for this approach is shown in the following illustration. The parsed directory is closed because we don't need to see what Fusebox builds—just the parts we're responsible for writing.

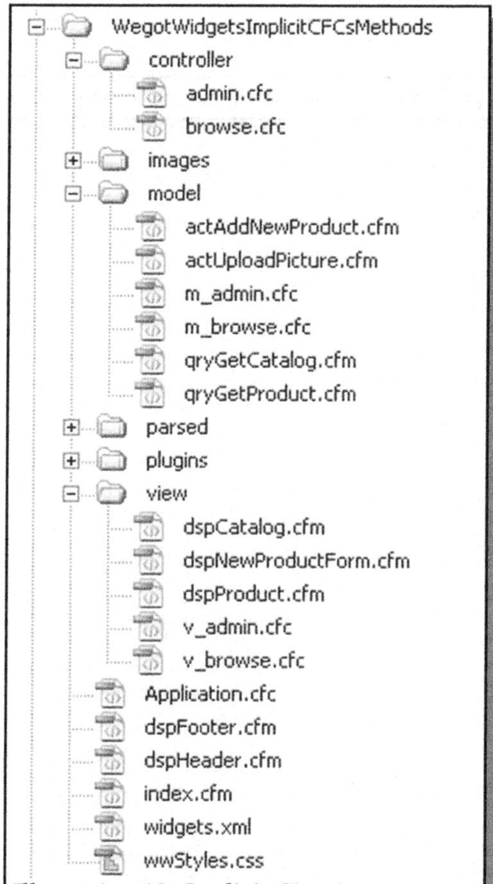

Illustration 19: Implicit Circuit Directories with Fuseaction CFM Files

Even though the logical circuits remain the same as the other samples in this book, the directories are different. The model, view and controller directories are special directories to Fusebox, allowing implicit circuits to be found within them. The following sections discuss how the application's critical parts work, starting with the application configuration.

Application Configuration

Since there's no fusebox.xml file, the application configuration relies on conventions rather than a configuration file. As with any ColdFusion application, we start with index.cfm, and Application.cfm or Application.cfc. In the case of this sample app, the work is handled in Application.cfc.

NOTE: Index.cfm is still required as the target for all calls in the application. However, it can be a zero-byte file.

```
<!--- index.cfm for WegotWidgetsImplicitCFCsMethods --->

<!--- Application.cfc for WegotWidgetsImplicitCFCsMethods --->
<cfcomponent extends="fusebox5.Application" output="false">
   <!--- trap non-index.cfm requests - must be outside onXxxYyy() handlers --->
   <cfif right(cgi.script_name, len("index.cfm")) neq "index.cfm" and right(cgi.script_name, 3) neq "cfc">
      <cflocation url="index.cfm" addtoken="no" />
   </cfif>

   <!--- set application name based on the directory path --->
   <cfset this.name = right(REReplace(expandPath('.'),'[^A-Za-z]','','all'),64) />
   <cfset this.sessionManagement = true />

   <cfscript>
      FUSEBOX_PARAMETERS.allowImplicitFusebox = true;
      FUSEBOX_PARAMETERS.defaultFuseaction = "browse.showCatalog";
      FUSEBOX_PARAMETERS.mode = "development-full-load";
      FUSEBOX_PARAMETERS.conditionalParse = true;
      // change this to something more secure:
      FUSEBOX_PARAMETERS.password = "";
      FUSEBOX_PARAMETERS.strictMode = true;
      FUSEBOX_PARAMETERS.debug = true;
      // we use the core file error templates:
      FUSEBOX_PARAMETERS.errortemplatesPath = "/fusebox551/errortemplates/";
   </cfscript>

   <cffunction name="onFuseboxApplicationStart">
    <cfset super.onFuseboxApplicationStart() />
    <cfset dsn="WegotWidgets" />
     <cfset self="index.cfm" />
     <cfset myself="#self#?fuseaction=" />
   </cffunction>

   <cffunction name="onRequestStart">
    <cfargument name="targetPage" />
    <cfset super.onRequestStart(arguments.targetPage) />
     <cfinclude template="dspHeader.cfm">
   </cffunction>

  <cffunction name="onRequestEnd">
   <cfset super.onRequestEnd(arguments.targetPage) />
   <cfinclude template="dspHeader.cfm">
  </cffunction>
</cfcomponent>
```

In Application.cfc, there are a couple of important things to note. First is that the <cfcomponent> tag extends the Fusebox application component. We'll look at this again in a later section. Second, the Fusebox-related configuration code falls in the component's initialization section—before any <cffunction> blocks. The <cfscript> block sets up the

Fusebox parameters that would have been defined in fusebox.xml. Because we're not defining circuits with an explicit fusebox.xml file, the allowImplicitFusebox parameter must be set to **true**.

Finally, as with the sample in the previous chapter, the application uses the OnRequestStart and OnRequestEnd methods to present a header and footer. Rather than using fuseactions, they are just included as CFML templates in their respective methods. As such, the header and footer can be viewed as being outside the Fusebox application. Instead, they are treated somewhat as wrappers for the entire application. In a more complex application, we would use content variables and a layout fuseaction to present the final layout.

Default Fuseaction

As it would be if we were using fusebox.xml, the default fuseaction is set with the defaultFuseaction parameter. The difference in the no-XML is that this parameter is set in CFML instead of in XML. The choice to place the CFML in Appliction.cfc is arbitrary. We could just as well have chosen to use index.cfm or Application.cfm for the same purpose.

Parameters

As shown in the code section, the Fusebox parameters are also set in CFML instead of in XML. The only caveat is to make sure parameters are set before the Fusebox core is called. Since we're using Application.cfc, which extends the Fusebox application CFC, the parameters are set in the CFC's initialization section, before any <cffunction> declarations.

Circuit Definition

Circuit definition is the most obvious difference between the traditional modern approach to Fusebox and the no-XML approach. Without a fusebox.xml file, there is no <circuits> section to set up the circuit/alias configuration.

Fusebox 5.5 could have taken an approach similar to versions of Fusebox prior to 4, using CFML to set up the circuit definitions. But Sean made a decision to have the Fusebox 5.5 framework be a little more helpful to developers. So instead of just substituting a CFML-based version of circuit definition for the XML, Fusebox 5.5 figures out what the circuits are all by itself.

The details of how Fusebox does this are found in Chapter 4. For this particular sample application, the circuits are CFCs under the special directories “controller”, “model”, and “view”. So when a fuseaction with a circuit of **browse** is requested, Fusebox sees that a

CFC named “browse.cfc” exists under the controller directory, and uses that directory as the circuit. If a fuseaction is called for which no circuit can be deduced, Fusebox will throw a “circuit not defined” error.

Initialization

The Fusebox framework is initialized in this approach by the fact that Application.cfc extends the Fusebox application CFC. The code that falls within Application.cfc before any <cffunction> blocks constitutes the application's initialization code.

Fuseaction Definition

In this particular sample, fuseactions are defined by CFC methods, one for each fuseaction. When using this approach, each CFC has a function for each fuseaction in the circuit, named for that fuseaction. This sample's CFC files are shown below. Keep in mind that there are controller, model, and view circuits for each logical circuit.

```
<!--- controller/admin.cfc --->
<cfcomponent access="public">
  <cffunction name="addNewProduct">
    <cfargument name="myFusebox" />
    <cfargument name="event" />
    <cfset myFusebox.do("m_admin.actAddNewProduct") />
    <cfset myFusebox.do("browse.showCatalog") />
  </cffunction>
  <cffunction name="showNewProductForm">
    <cfargument name="myFusebox" />
    <cfargument name="event" />
    <cfset event.xfa("submitForm","admin.addNewProduct") />
    <cfset myFusebox.do("v_admin.dspNewProductForm") />
  </cffunction>
</cfcomponent>

<!--- controller/browse.cfc --->
<cfcomponent access="public">
  <cffunction name="showProduct">
    <cfargument name="myFusebox" />
    <cfargument name="event" />
    <cfset event.xfa("lnkBackToCatalog","browse.showCatalog")>
    <cfset event.qryGetProduct = myFusebox.do("m_browse.qryGetProduct") />
    <cfset myFusebox.do("v_browse.dspProduct") />
  </cffunction>
  <cffunction name="showCatalog">
    <cfargument name="myFusebox" />
    <cfargument name="event" />
    <cfset event.xfa("lnkProductName","browse.showProduct") />
    <cfset event.xfa("lnkAdmin","admin.showNewProductForm") />
    <cfset event.qryGetCatalog = myFusebox.do("m_browse.qryGetCatalog") />
    <cfset myFusebox.do("v_browse.dspCatalog") />
  </cffunction>
</cfcomponent>

<!--- model/m_admin.cfc --->
<cfcomponent access="internal">
  <cffunction name="actAddNewProduct">
    <cfargument name="myFusebox" />
    <cfargument name="event" />
    <cfinclude template="actUploadPicture.cfm">
    <cfinclude template="actAddNewProduct.cfm">
  </cffunction>
</cfcomponent>

<!--- model/m_browse.cfc --->
<cfcomponent access="internal">
  <cffunction name="qryGetProduct">
    <cfargument name="myFusebox" />
    <cfargument name="event" />
```

```
    <cfinclude template="qryGetProduct.cfm">
    <cfset event.setValue("qryGetProduct", qryGetProduct)>
  </cffunction>
  <cffunction name="qryGetCatalog">
    <cfargument name="myFusebox" />
    <cfargument name="event" />
    <cfinclude template="qryGetCatalog.cfm">
    <cfset event.setValue("qryGetCatalog", qryGetCatalog)>
  </cffunction>
</cfcomponent>

<!--- view/v_admin.cfc --->
<cfcomponent access="internal">
  <cffunction name="dspNewProductForm">
    <cfargument name="myFusebox" />
    <cfargument name="event" />
    <cfset attributes = myFusebox.variables()>
    <cfinclude template="dspNewProductForm.cfm">
  </cffunction>
</cfcomponent>

<!--- view/v_browse.cfc --->
<cfcomponent access="internal">
  <cffunction name="dspCatalog">
    <cfargument name="myFusebox" />
    <cfargument name="event" />
    <cfset attributes = myFusebox.variables()>
    <cfset qryGetCatalog = attributes.attributes.qryGetCatalog>
    <cfinclude template="dspCatalog.cfm">
  </cffunction>
  <cffunction name="dspProduct">
    <cfargument name="myFusebox" />
    <cfargument name="event" />
    <cfset attributes = myFusebox.variables()>
    <cfset qryGetProduct = attributes.attributes.qryGetProduct>
    <cfinclude template="dspProduct.cfm">
  </cffunction>
</cfcomponent>
```

This approach to fuseaction configuration appeals to developers who are comfortable with CFCs. It is the approach that would be used if we wanted to instantiate objects to represent data constructs from the model. Although the model in this application doesn't feature CFCs that represent data constructs as a more object-oriented application would, it takes advantage of the difference between public and internal components to provide added security and robustness. It also allows the architect to work in CFCs while the fuse programmers still work in plain old CFML fuse files.

Summary

This sample application demonstrates the use of implicit circuits defined by ColdFusion Components, with fuseactions implied by the use of methods within those components. Fusebox parameters are set in Application.cfc, though Application.cfm or index.cfm could also be used (see other sample chapters). The Fusebox framework is initialized by using Application.cfc to extend the Fusebox application component. Each fuseaction is defined with its own CFC method named for that fuseaction.

This is the end of our chapters with sample variations of the Wegot Widgets application. Though by no means an exhaustive demonstration of the techniques available in Fusebox 5.5, these samples should provide enough exposure to the various "no-XML" (and semi-XML) approaches to serve as a strong springboard into further exploration.

Chapter 10 – Summary

Contrary to its designation as a point release, Fusebox 5.5 represents a significant move forward in the history of Fusebox. Where the "traditional modern" approach to Fusebox (my designation for the use of XML-based configuration files for the application and circuits) makes extensive use of XML, Fusebox 5.5 introduces support for the full Fusebox framework without the use of XML configuration files.

In place of XML configuration, Fusebox 5.5 allows the use of implicit circuits defined by directory names or CFC names. The approaches can even be mixed within an application, though this is not a recommended practice.

With no application configuration file (fusebox.xml), the application configuration chores are relocated into CFML in any of several places. Choices include index.cfm, Application.cfc, or Application.cfm, depending on which approach is used. Fusebox parameters, including the default fuseaction, are set in this manner.

Circuit definition (i.e., fuseaction specification) chores in Fusebox 5.5 are handled in one of several ways, depending on which approach for circuits has been used. For implicit circuits defined by directory name, fuseactions can be created using CFML templates, CFCs, and even circuit.xml. Though the Fusebox 5.5 specification called for the ability to use XML templates for each fuseaction, this approach has not been enabled in the framework as of this writing. For implicit circuits defined by CFC, fuseactions are created using methods within the circuit CFCs. All of the fuseaction creation techniques available for implicit circuits defined by directory name are also available for explicit circuits defined by fusebox.xml. This indicates the degree of flexibility available in Fusebox 5.5.

When doing without XML configuration files, several issues must be considered. These issues include replacing the functionality of fusebox.xml (including setting the Fusebox parameters and defining circuits), replacing the functionality of circuit.xml, and implicitly locating circuits.

Fusebox 5.5 also provides a number of new capabilities that are not directly related to the elimination of XML configuration files. These capabilities include the dynamic do, the event object, Application.cfc support, and debug trace improvements. There is also a new shortcut method, myFusebox.getApplicationData().

The Wegot Widgets reference application for Fusebox is used to provide a common ground for discussion of Fusebox-related topics. This book presents four variants of the Wegot Widgets application: using directories as circuits with circuit.xml to define fuseactions; using directories as circuits with CFML templates as fuseactions, using directories as circuits with CFCs as fuseactions, and using CFCs as circuits with methods as fuseactions.

This book is designed to be a reasonable overview of Fusebox 5.5, with enough technical detail to allow developers to leverage its new capabilities quickly. There are plenty of additional resources for Fusebox 5.5 available, most of which can be found on the Fusebox website at www.Fusebox.org.

The appendices also provide some additional reference material to help you on your Fusebox travels. They include a Fusebox glossary and more information on additional Fusebox resources.

Appendix A - Fusebox Glossary

action fuse – a template that does not present any data to the user, or interact with the database. Usually has act_ as its prefix. For more information, see Chapter 3 "Fusebox Framework Files".

application configuration file – the XML file where circuits, parameters, global fuseactions, and plugins are defined (fusebox.xml.cfm).

architect – the person responsible for the development of a Fusebox application. Oversees the entire project, and is responsible for circuit design and Fusedocs.

circuit – a collection of fuseactions. Circuits are groups of program behavior arranged due to common behavior. For example, all fuseactions having to do with management of user accounts might be placed in a circuit called Users. Deciding which fuseactions belong in which circuits is part of the architect's job. For more information, see Chapter 3 "Fusebox Framework Files".

circuit configuration file – the XML file where fuseactions are defined for a circuit (circuit.xml.cfm).

component content variable (CCV) – a variable that holds some generated content for use within a Fusebox site.

core file – the file that handles the "heavy lifting" central to Fusebox processing. There are four core files in Fusebox 4: the Runtime, the Loader, the Transformer, and the Parser.

designer – the person responsible for the visual design of a Fusebox application.

dynamic do – calling a fuseaction within code. Introduced in Fusebox 5.5.

event object – a construct that enables some Fusebox 5 features, including a pointer to the variables scope of the application.

exit fuseaction (XFA) – a variable that contains a fuseaction that may be used to exit a given fuse. For example, if a fuse uses a button named Save, the architect might create an XFA named XFA.btnSave, with the value "users.saveUser" stored in it. This allows fuses to be coded with variable destinations, e.g., `fuseaction=#XFA.btnSave#`", instead of being hard-coded.

exit point - A place where processing leaves a fuse, such as a form action or redirection.

FLiP – Fusebox Lifecycle Process: a web development methodology that includes wireframes, prototypes, DevNotes, formalized architecture, distributed coding, and unit testing.

front end – sometimes used to refer to a prototype. Because a Fusebox prototype becomes the front end for the finished application, this term is often used when talking to clients.

fuse – an individual code file that contributes to processing a fuseaction. One or more fuses may contribute to a fuseaction. Typically divided into display, action, query, and sometimes url categories.

fuse file – the file that holds a fuse. In ColdFusion, a fuse file is a single CFML template.

fuseaction – a collection of fuses that perform an action within a Fusebox application. For example, a fuseaction might consist of a query fuse to fetch data from a database and a display fuse to present the data to the user. Every request in a Fusebox 4 application employs at least one fuseaction.

Fuseboxer – a person who uses Fusebox.

fusecoder – a person who writes the code for a fuse, as specified in its Fusedoc.

Fusedoc – a specification for documenting the inputs and outputs to be used by a fuse. Also refers to the documentation block at the top of a fuse file. The architect is responsible for creating the Fusedoc, and a fusecoder is responsible for writing the fuse's code according to its Fusedoc.

home circuit – The top-level circuit in a Fusebox application. Also called the main circuit.

MVC – Model View Controller. A design pattern which separates code in terms of its job: either having to do with the data (model), its presentation to the user (view), or the relationship between those two (controller). Fusebox itself uses an implicit MVC approach by recommending the separation of query, display, and action fuses; a more rigorous and explicit approach involves the use of directories named "model", "view" and "controller".

query fuse – a template that interacts with the database. Usually has qry_ as its prefix.

target circuit – in the context of a fuseaction, the circuit in which the requested fuseaction is located.

XFA - see exit fuseaction

Appendix B – Fusebox Resources

Several categories of great resources are available to Fusebox developers. The first and perhaps foremost of these is the community. Fuseboxers are a great bunch of folks, with all kinds of experience to offer. The best place to meet up with them is on the Fusebox forums and the Fusebox Community mail list.

- **Fusebox.org and Fusebox Forums** – The Official Fusebox Site is the home of the latest Fusebox specification. You can also find supporting information such as whitepapers, presentations, sample code, and links to other resources. This is the site to visit if you're interested in formally participating in the future of Fusebox. The forums are located at http://www.fusebox.org/forums/

- **Fusebox Yahoo Group (http://tech.groups.yahoo.com/group/fusebox5/)**-- This is probably the most popular Fusebox forum/mail list.

You can also find plenty of information at various Fusebox-related web sites:

Community Sites

The Fusebox community is the primary support mechanism for most Fuseboxers. Several sites are available with information from current and past versions of Fusebox.

- **www.corfield.org (Sean Corfield)**--Sean is the driving force behind Fusebox 5, and his site and blog "An Architect's View" are regular brainfood for most Fuseboxers.
- **www.halhelms.com (Hal Helms)**--Hal's site has several areas, including some of his writing and a collection of the code he has discussed in various venues.
- **www.grokfusebox.com (Jeff Peters)**--GrokFusebox.com is about "getting it." You will find links to resources about Fusebox and ColdFusion in general.
- Community resources at fusebox.org: **http://www.fusebox.org/go/fusebox-community/community-resources**

Commercial Sites

Some companies have been instrumental in Fusebox's rise to the forefront of ColdFusion development. Among the most active are these:

- **TeraTech (www.teratech.com)**--TeraTech is a Washington, D.C.-based company that provides development services and training in ColdFusion and Fusebox. TeraTech's president is Michael Smith, whose work you might have read in ColdFusion Developer's Journal. TeraTech is currently the gatekeeper organization for Fusebox.
- **Fusebuilder (www.fusebuilder.com)** – A longtime supporter of Fusebox and source of Fusebox-related tools. Fusebuilder's founder, Mike Ritchie, maintains the PHP version of the Fusebox core. Their mailing list can be reached through PHP-fusebox@yahoogroups.com.

Other Fusebox Books

There are now several Fusebox-related books on the market. Though the usual search at your favorite book site will turn up some of these, several are only available on the publisher's site.

- **Proton Arts (www.protonarts.com)**--Proton Arts has published my last 9 books. Some titles are only available through the web site and a limited number of bookstores (such as Reiter's Scientific Bookstore in Washington, DC).
- **Techspedition (www.techspedition.com)**--Techspedition Fusebox 3/4 and general ColdFusion titles. Books available on Amazon.com as well.
- Fusebox: Developing ColdFusion Applications (Peters and Papovich, New Riders)--covers Fusebox 3 and the Fusebox Lifecycle Process (FLiP). Availble from Amazon.com.
- Fusebox : Methodology & Techniques, ColdFusion Edition (Nelson and Girard, Fusion Authority)--The first Fusebox book published. Now mostly a collector's item, but if you want the complete story, this book is still on Amazon.com

You Be the Resource

Of course, you can be a great resource, too. Set up a site, offer some cool stuff, and let the community know about it.

Alphabetical Index

Illustration Index

Made in the USA
Monee, IL
08 November 2026

68020215R00063